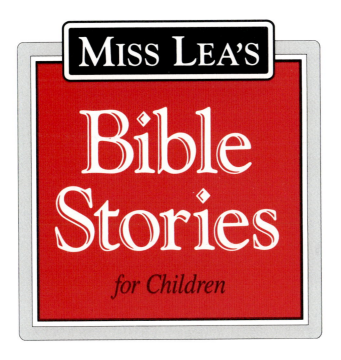

MISS LEA'S

Bible
Stories

for Children

Written by
Rosemary Lea

Illustrated by
Stephen Sechrist

ZAGAT SURVEY ■ NEW YORK

To the boys of St. Bernard's
who inspired these stories

2ND PRINTING

ISBN: 1-57006-003-7
First Edition

Published by Zagat Survey, 4 Columbus Circle, New York, NY 10019

ABOUT THE AUTHOR

Rosemary Lea was born in 1927 in Worcestershire, England. After being educated at home by family and tutors, Miss Lea worked as a governess and tutor for years. In 1963, she moved to New York City, where, except for one year studying for her Masters Degree in Education at Harvard University, she has been a teacher at St. Bernard's School. This is Miss Lea's first writing venture.

CONTENTS

FOREWORD

It has been roughly twelve years since we first met Miss Lea. Saying we "met her" isn't exactly correct. Actually, we observed her, and only briefly, but she made a strong impression on us.

We were taking our then five-year-old son Teddy to see elementary schools to decide where he would go after "graduating" from kindergarten. One of the schools we visited was St. Bernard's, where he and his younger brother John both ended up. It was there on our inspection tour that we were shown into the first grade class being taught by Rosemary Lea.

We didn't know her name then, of course. We just stood in the doorway and observed a very erect, middle-aged teacher with steel-gray bangs who spoke a distinctly upper-class English. But it wasn't her accent that was most remarkable — it was what she said and how she said it. "Boy!" she exclaimed to a pint-sized towhead, "don't be so foolish. You know you can't go to the bathroom in the middle of reading period." Noticing us at the door she turned and said, "Boys are like puppies — one goes, and they all want to go. We'd never get any reading done!" Then her gaze returned to the boys. "Now, has anyone got something brilliant to say, or shall we get on with the story? Or would you like me to bang all your heads together for some fun?"

That was about all we saw of Miss Lea before our St. Bernard's escort brought us to observe another class. "Who is that teacher?" we inquired warily. The answer came quickly: "Miss Lea — she's not as tough as she looks. The boys love her."

We had to wait nearly a year before we learned how true that was. But during that time we began to worry: What if our dear little boy is assigned to Miss Lea's class — could he take it? What would happen if he needed to go to the bathroom and couldn't wait until the end of the lesson? We finally decided there wasn't any reason to worry. Since there were three sections in the first grade, the odds were two-to-one in our favor that he would get another teacher.

But when we arrived for our son's first day at St. Bernard's, there was his name under the feared heading: "First Grade — Lea." Fortunately, on the first day of school, the boys had to go upstairs with their teachers for only one hour, while we parents were subjected to indoctrination speeches. We waited anxiously for our little darling to come down — ready, if need be, to request a change of class assignment. When he came back down, he didn't look any the worse for wear. "How was your new teacher?" we asked anxiously. He responded without hesitation, "Terrific!"

Now after almost twelve years, through the eyes of two very different sons and through the experience of their friends who were lovingly excoriated by Miss Lea, we know that our elder son's first reaction was right — Miss Lea *is* terrific.

Through her brisk, no-nonsense manner, the boys immediately sensed a kindness that was nothing short of love — love both for them and for the process that was to take them from illiteracy to reading competence, in one short school year.

Miss Lea insisted that we as parents read to and be read to in turn by our sons, if possible, every first-grade night. Not only did we share our sons' progress to literacy in this way, but it enriched our relationship with them as well.

One other thing that Miss Lea taught was the Bible. She would regularly tell Bible stories to the boys — not just the boys from her class but to the whole lower school at their weekly assembly — starting with the Creation and going on to the story of Tobit. One thing was clear: Both of our boys loved hearing these wonderful tales.

Recently, Miss Lea taped recordings of her Bible stories, and we bought the tapes. To our surprise and pleasure, we found our sons going to bed listening to her clipped, very English renderings of these Bible stories.

Only recently did it occur to us to ask Miss Lea if she had transcribed her Bible stories, and indeed she had.

What follows is Miss Lea's version of the Bible stories that she has told to innumerable St. Bernard's boys over the past thirty years. We hope you will enjoy reading some of the greatest stories ever told to your own children.

Nina and Tim Zagat

PREFACE

When I was a child I lived deep in the English countryside, in Worcestershire toward the Welsh border. We were a family of five children, and for much of the time, the Second World War was going on. There was no television. We did not go to the movies. (There was no spare petrol at all for going anywhere for fun, and anyway we scarcely knew movies existed.) We did not go to school, we did all our lessons at home. (This is a very good way of learning a great deal, by the way, because you do not have to sit and wait while some of the children in the class have to have things explained several times!) No one ever locked anything up — not their houses, not their cars, not their bicycles, in fact, not anything. It was about as different from growing up in New York City as life on the *Mayflower.*

But we did have books — many, many wonderful books — and we all read constantly, both in and out of the schoolroom. In our schoolroom we read Shakespeare, Scott, Dickens and many others. And, of course, the Bible. Even before we could read, the Bible stories were well known to us, told to us by our mother. In the schoolroom, we learnt by heart reams of Bible verses (needless to say, from the King James Bible, which is why I feel so uncomfortable with the modern, emasculated language in the new translations.)

It was when I graduated from Bible storybooks to the real Bible that I realized how human and rascally — nay downright wicked indeed — some of the characters in the Old Testament were, not at all the rather sanctimonious people they had been portrayed as. I retold myself these stories in this new guise and compared them with the pantheon of Greek and Norse gods, all of whom we read about as well.

Many, many years later I found myself at St. Bernard's School, in New York City, in charge of teaching first graders in the Junior School section, which was then under the rule of Andrew McLaren. I found that many of the boys did not know the stories of the Bible and idly mentioned this to Mr. McLaren. "Let us do something about it," said he, and then and there began the tradition of telling Bible stories once a week to the assembled Junior School boys. At first he and I took it in turns; but very soon he said he was too busy, and ever since then, with scarcely a break, I have done this story-telling.

Two of these stories — Daniel and Bel, and Daniel and the Dragon — come from a part of the Bible known as the Apocrypha, which comes from a Greek word meaning "hidden away." Long ago when wise people were collecting these old stories, they were unsure about a number of them. Were they true? Or were they very good stories that were perhaps a bit exaggerated? Because they were not completely sure about them, they put them in a special section and called it the Apocrypha. Nowadays people will say things like, "Oh have you heard this one? I don't know if it's strictly true; it might be apocryphal, but it's a good story." I have included these two about Daniel because though there might be doubt about them, they are very good stories.

Quite apart from being among the best stories in the world, it seems to me that no one could be considered educated or cultured who is unaware of them. They also, along with Shakespeare, cover the whole gamut of human behavior and growth, and much can be learnt from them, all unawares. At one point I doubted this, though, when, after I had told the story of Jacob and Rachel, one teacher said she had taken her class upstairs and asked who could tell her the name of Jacob's favorite wife. Up went a hand instantly, and the reply came, "Churchill."

From time to time when I reach the end of these stories, I tell the tale of Pilgrim's Progress, but minus the moralizing. I explain about allegories at the beginning and leave it to them to discover what I call "the secret meanings," or just to enjoy the tale. Once, some weeks after I had finished, a first grader said to me, "Do you know what your Apollyon is, Miss Lea? I know what mine is." I felt he more than made up for Churchill.

During my years as a first-grade teacher, the boys in my class also memorized reams of lines, acting out these stories as plays. These and the stories were all listened to with undivided attention. Indeed, is there any more enjoyable occupation than being told a good story? What is more exciting than Shadrach, Meshach and Abednego in the burning, fiery furnace? Or more satisfying than little David defeating huge Goliath? When is just retribution more deserved than when Esther turns the tables on Haman? So I hope the stories in this book will give you as much pleasure as they have given to nearly thirty years of St. Bernard's boys.

Rosemary Lea

INTRODUCTION

The Bible is in two parts: the Old Testament and the New Testament. These stories come from the Old Testament. They are really not only Jewish history stories but also the history of the Jews' — and later the Christians' — search for God.

The stories start about four or five thousand years ago. That's a long, long time ago. Before then people had lots of gods. There were gods for everything you can imagine — and goddesses, too. There was a god for the sun, another for the moon; there were gods and goddesses for things like rain, thunder, crops. There were gods for rivers, trees, animals and homes. Sometimes even the kings were said to be gods.

It was the Jews who had the idea that there was probably only one God who was in charge of everything, and the Bible shows what they thought He was like, and how their ideas about Him changed with time.

Ever since there have been people, there have been stories about the way the world began, so there are many different ideas about it. The story at the very beginning of the Old Testament is about the way the Jews said the world was made by God, and that is the story I am starting with.

These are not all the stories in the Bible. There are many others, including, in the New Testament, those about Jesus. But I tell these particular ones, not only because they are splendid stories, but also because of the thread of history that runs through so many of them. We cannot see the pattern or reason for our own lives as we live them, but I do believe there is one. And by reading these stories, it is possible to see the "just because of" and "if this hadn't happened" of the lives of these people. Just think. If Jacob had not stolen Esau's blessing, he would probably never have gone to his uncle, fallen in love with Rachel, and been made to marry Leah first. If he hadn't spoiled Rachel's son Joseph so outrageously, Joseph might never have annoyed his ten older brethren. He would not have been sold to the Egyptian traders, he would not have had a chance to tell Pharaoh the meaning of his dreams: many of the Egyptians, and many of Jacob and Joseph's family, would all have starved to death in the famine years. The Children of Israel would never have gone to live in Goshen. They would never have been turned into slaves by the Egyptians, and there would, above all, have been no Moses, no David and no Jesus. What a very different world we would be living in now!

In any event, these stories can be read for their historic interest, for help in understanding our human endeavors, or just for plain fun and interest. I hope you enjoy them as much as I have through my life.

PART ONE

The Creation

I n the beginning God made heaven and earth, but there was nothing alive on the earth and everywhere was pitch dark. So one day as the spirit of God was moving around on the waters, He said, "Well, really, it's a great deal too dark around here. I can't see a thing I'm doing. Let's have some light."

So immediately it grew light, and God said, "That's simply excellent, but let's not have it light the whole time — it might get tedious. Let's halve it."

So He called the light part "day" and the dark part "night" and He approved of what He'd done. And that was the first day and the first night.

The second day, as He looked around again, God said, "Yes, so far so good, but there's too much water everywhere. Let's have some land as well."

So land appeared, and God looked at it and said, "Yes, that's what I mean. That's excellent."

On the third day, as God looked about the place, He said, "Now we're getting somewhere. I'm really enjoying this. Now let's have lots of grass and flowers and trees, and fruit and lovely colors to make the earth beautiful. All this brown is boring."

So green grass, beautiful flowers, trees and color came to the earth, and God said, "That is just great."

On the fourth day, God got the lighting properly organized, with the sun doing all the daytime work and the moon giving smaller nighttime light with millions of brilliant stars to help it. And He decided He was doing exactly the right thing.

The fifth day, as He looked at His work, He said, "Yes, yes, it is beautiful. Creating is fun. Now I think the moment has come to make living things that move, as well as ones with roots. I believe I shall start with sea animals and birds."

So He made fish — big fish and little fish — and enormous great whales, and birds to fly and sing. When He'd finished He looked at them and said, "You'll do. Now get busy multiplying yourselves and filling up the seas and trees."

On the sixth day, God said, "I really think I've almost finished. What we need now is something living on the land."

So He made elephants, lions, giraffes, tigers, hippopotamuses, cows, pigs, horses, sheep, snakes, worms, rats, mice, ants, spiders and butterflies, and all the other animals there are. And when He took a look He said, "My goodness, how marvelous! That's just what I had in mind. Now the last creature I need to make is a man to take charge of all this for me."

So God breathed on some dust and made a man with a living soul.

"There," said God. "I have really worked exceedingly hard and made an exquisite world. I shall rest now."

And on the seventh day God had a rest.

The Garden of Eden

The most beautiful part of God's beautiful new world was a garden called, of course, the Garden of Eden. And in this beautiful garden God put the new man to live. And He called the new man Adam. It was Adam's job to look after the garden. It was also Adam's job to give names to all the animals.

"You can call them whatever you like," said God. "Whatever name you pick for them, that will be their name."

So that gave Adam something to do for quite a long time, thinking up names for the hundreds of kinds of animals God had made. But after a while he came to the end of the animals — and probably to the end of the names he could invent too — and though he found gardening interesting, Adam began to feel lonely.

So that evening, as he had his regular daily talk with God about how things were going, Adam said, "Everything is going very well, but to be honest I'm getting lonely. Though it's marvelous to talk to you every evening, I know you're very busy, and I'd really rather like someone to talk to during the daytime and help with the weeding and so on."

"All right," said God. "I'll see what I can think up for you."

And that evening while Adam was sleeping happily, God took one of Adam's ribs and made it into a wife for him.

"Here is a helper for you," said God. "She is called Eve and will keep you company. And by the way, you can both eat all the fruit you want in this place. It is there to be eaten. But you may not eat the fruit from that tree in the middle there, that tree of knowledge. If you do, you will immediately find out a whole lot of things it would be much less trouble not to know, such as the difference between good and bad, glad and sad, youth and age, life and death, courage and cowardice. You will also have to start making decisions, making meals and goodness knows what else besides. In short, just give that tree a miss, all right?"

"Oh, certainly," said Adam and Eve. "There are plenty of other things to eat without eating from the tree of knowledge."

So Adam and Eve lived a peaceful, uneventful life until one ill-fated day. Eve was walking about by herself, without enough to do, when what should she meet but a serpent. Now a serpent is another name for a snake, and this particular serpent was a thorough snake-in-the-grass.

"Hello, Eve," he said smoothly. "And how are you today?"

"Oh, I'm all right, thank you," she said. "But I'm a bit bored, you know. There doesn't seem to be much to do, and Adam's not about just now."

"Ah, yes," said the snake in a sly voice. "Well, why don't you try one of these luscious fruits to pass the time? I'd love to know what they taste like."

"Oh, no," Eve said. "This is the fruit God said we mustn't eat, you know."

"Well, God doesn't seem to be around now, either, so you could take a tiny weeny bite without Him knowing. Go on, I dare you."

So Eve said, "I suppose you're right. It couldn't matter if I took just a small taste."

With that she took a bite and found it was the most delectable fruit she had ever tasted.

Just then along came Adam.

"Eve," he said, "what *are* you doing? That's the fruit God said we weren't supposed to eat; whatever will He say?"

"Well, I was bored," said Eve, "and anyway it's delicious. You try some."

So then they both ate some, and it was unbelievably good. But when they'd finished, they both felt an entirely new feeling. They felt as if they'd done something wrong. They had, of course, and their consciences had come alive.

"Oh, dear," said Adam. "I have a feeling God won't be exactly pleased about this. I'm not much looking forward to our evening talk, are you?"

"No," Eve said. "Why don't we hide and not talk to Him? If He doesn't see us, perhaps He'll go away."

But naturally such a foolish plan was doomed to failure. As soon as evening came, God took his usual walk through the garden, and as soon as He knew that Adam and Eve were hiding, He knew just what had happened, and He most decidedly was *not* exactly pleased about it.

"Didn't I clearly tell you *not* to eat that fruit?" He asked Adam. "Why do you do the only thing I told you *not* to do?"

Adam weakly blamed his wife.

"Eve made me do it," he said.

Eve equally weakly blamed the snake.

"The snake made me do it," she said. "I couldn't help it."

"Nonsense," said God. "You are both quite old enough to take your own blame; you're not babies any more. So now you can't live in this garden any longer. Now that you've started finding things out, you must go out into the world and go on finding things out whether you like it or not, as a punishment; and the snake's punishment is to crawl about on his stomach forevermore."

"Oh, bother," thought the snake, "how too horribly dusty, and all for an old bit of fruit."

Thus began the trials and tribulations of the world. And God put cherubim to guard the way into Eden, and a flaming sword turning in all directions around the tree of knowledge.

Cain and Abel

O ne of the things that Adam and Eve soon found out was not all fun and games was bringing up children. First they had a son called Cain and then another one called Abel. Cain looked after the crops and Abel looked after the sheep; but instead of being friends with each other, Cain was very jealous of Abel. Perhaps he thought his mother spoiled him.

Now ever since the Garden of Eden had been put out of bounds, they were not always sure if God was listening. So they decided to build a little fire, and if the smoke went straight up to heaven, they assumed God was listening. If the smoke swirled about messily, they thought God was annoyed and not listening to them at all. What part they imagined the wind played, goodness knows.

Be that as it may, there came a day when Cain and Abel were out in the fields together at prayer time, and both built suitable little fires. But Cain began having trouble with his smoke.

"The wretched stuff," he thought. "Why won't my smoke go up straight? Why isn't God paying any attention to me?"

Then he happened to look across at Abel's smoke and what did he see? Why, the smoke going up absolutely dead straight, of course. This made Cain utterly furious.

"That horrible young brother of mine," he muttered. "First our mother spoils him and now God does. It's really going too far."

And in a fit of terrible temper, Cain killed Abel. Whereupon God spoke to him instantly, so He'd obviously been listening all the time.

"Ah, good evening, Cain," He said. "And where is your brother Abel today?"

"Good heavens, how should I know?" lied Cain crossly. "Am I my brother's keeper?"

"Yes, you are," said God, "and I happen to know you've killed him. So now I fear you are cursed and must wander the earth for the rest of your life."

So Cain went with his wife to a land called Nod, and they had a son called Enoch and began a city, which he called Enoch too. Perhaps Cain was not as good at thinking up names as his father was.

Luckily, Eve had another son called Seth who was thoroughly satisfactory. It was Seth's descendant who was called Noah, and Noah is the hero of the next story.

Noah's Ark

Many hundreds of years passed, and the land was thickly peopled by the descendants of Adam and Eve. And a most unruly, unsatisfactory bunch they were too. They had nearly all forgotten about God and had given up their evening talks with Him, and had done all the wicked things you can think of. God wished He'd never had the idea of making people, and He decided He would get rid of them. But then, as he looked around, He saw one family that was not wicked and had not forgotten Him.

"Ha!" said God. "I'll get rid of them all except Noah and his family. I'll save them."

So God went to Noah and said, "Look, Noah. I'm sick of all these wicked people, and I'm going to get rid of them. I shall send down a huge mass of rain until there's a flood, and I'll simply drown the whole lot of them. If you don't want to drown too, you'd better build an ark with room for you and your wife and your sons and their wives and children and two of every animal and bird, and get ready to be saved."

Then He gave Noah very careful instructions about the length, breadth, width, and height of the ark he had to build. And he told him to put in only one window, which doesn't seem very many for all those animals and people inside; but perhaps in all the rain it wouldn't make much difference.

So Noah started hammering and sawing, and his three sons — Ham, Shem and Japheth — helped.

The neighbors must have thought Noah had gone crazy, and they laughed him to scorn.

"Poor old Noah, he's really not as bright as he was. Have you heard the latest?"

"No, what? Tell us all."

"Well he says there's going to be a flood, and God has told him to make a whopping big ark to save his family and some animals from drowning. Did you ever hear such rubbish? Really, Noah and his old God. It makes me laugh."

But Noah was not as stupid as he looked. No sooner was the ark built, provisioned and filled with animals, than down came the pouring rain and in went Noah with his wife, sons, daughters-in-law and grandchildren, and God shut the door.

It rained for forty days and forty nights, and the whole place was under water until even the mountains were covered. And the flood lasted a hundred and fifty days, so that altogether Noah and the animals were in the ark for nearly half a year. The ark must have been very well made, and what a lot of food they must have put in, too.

Then a nice drying wind began to blow, and the waters gradually receded until the ark came to rest on land again. But it wasn't very useful land, since it was the top of a mountain called Mount Ararat. Let's hope it was not a very pointed mountain.

After a while Noah opened the window of the ark and sent out a big black bird, a raven. But it was a strong bird and flew long enough and far enough to find a landing place and was never seen again. So then Noah sent out a gentle dove, but she found nowhere to rest and Noah took her back in. A few days later he sent her out again. This time she came back with an olive branch in her beak, so Noah knew the waters had gone down as far as the trees below the mountain.

A few days later when he let the dove out, she did not come back at all and God said to Noah, "It's all right now. You can all come out, and I've decided I won't flood the whole place ever again. Here's the sign of my promise. See it? I've made a rainbow. Every time there's a rainbow in the sky, I will be remembering my promise."

So they all came out of the ark and went back into the world. They put up their tents and everything got going again; and before long the place was well-populated. But with a few notable exceptions, people were every bit as hopeless as before. One of these exceptions was Abram, in Mesopotamia.

Sodom and Gomorrah

Abram always tried to do what he thought God wanted, and he remembered to talk to God at every opportunity. One day while they were talking, God said to Abram, "I've decided to get rid of those tiresome cities of Sodom and Gomorrah. The people there are really far too wild. But having promised no more floods, I think I shall have to resort to sending fire and brimstone down on them. That will teach them a rather good lesson, I fancy."

And Abram said, "Oh, I'm sure that's a splendid plan, but suppose there are some good people in those places? Are you going to destroy the good people with the evil ones? Suppose there might be fifty good people there, for instance. Would you save the place for fifty good people?"

"Oh, yes," said God. "If I can find fifty good people, then I'll save the place."

So then Abram said, "Please, forgive me for being tiresome, but after all, you are the Judge of the world and must do right. Suppose there are only forty-five good people, then what? Will you burn it up?"

"No," said God. "For forty-five people I'll save it."

Then Abram said, "Well, *please* don't be angry with me, but what if there are only forty good people?"

"I'll save it for forty," said God.

Then Abram, getting ever more nervous and worried, said, "Peradventure" (which means "perhaps"), "peradventure there shall be only thirty?"

"I won't destroy the place for thirty," said God.

"What about twenty?" said Abram.

"I won't destroy the place for twenty good people," said God.

"I'm so sorry to be a nuisance, and this is the very last time I'll bother you this evening, but suppose there are only ten good people in the city?" asked Abram.

And God said, "I will not destroy it for ten good people's sakes."

But the only good people they could find were Lot and his wife and two daughters. Lot was Abram's nephew, so perhaps that is why Abram was so keen on finding out how many good people he'd need to save the city. And because there were not enough, he told Lot to leave with his family before the place was burned, and God told them on *no* account to turn back to look at the blazing city.

So Lot and his family came forth from the city, and God rained down a mass of fire and brimstone on Sodom and Gomorrah; and they were all consumed.

But peradventure Lot's wife was not really good enough to be saved and did not really believe God. Anyway, she looked back at the flames and was instantly turned into a pillar of salt, and Lot and his daughters had to go on without her, and went and lived in a cave.

Abraham and Sarah

One day God said to Abram, "Pack up your tents and take your flocks and your wife and your camels and your servants and go toward the land of Canaan because I shall give that land to your descendants. I will make a great nation of you and I'll bless you. Anyone that blesses you I'll bless, too, and anyone who curses you I'll curse."

"Oh, thank you," said Abram.

So Abram took his wife, Sarai, and all his possessions and started off. And God said, "Lift up your eyes and look north, south, east and west because all the land you can see from here I shall give to your descendants. You'll have as many descendants as there are particles of dust. If anyone can count the dust, that's as many descendants as you'll have."

"That's lovely," said Abram, "but as a matter of fact, my wife and I haven't got any children, so how can I have any descendants?"

"Well, don't worry," said God. "It will be all right. I shall make nations and kings out of you. I promise you. And to remind you of this promise, from now on you shall be called Abraham and your wife shall be called Sarah."

It was very hard for Abraham and Sarah to believe this, because they'd wanted children for a very long time but had none. And they were quite old now. Sarah's Egyptian maid, Hagar, had a son called Ishmael, and Sarah was dreadfully jealous and began to hate them both.

The next time she heard God tell Abraham she'd have a son, she laughed to herself. When God asked her why she had laughed, she grew scared and said she hadn't.

"Well, never mind," said God. "You'll have a son in less than a year now."

And, sure enough, Sarah had a son and they called him Isaac. Everyone was delighted and they gave a great feast in their camp.

Hagar and Ishmael

For a while all went well. But do you remember Sarah's maid Hagar and her son Ishmael? Well, as Isaac grew from a baby into a boy, Ishmael kept on teasing him. No doubt Isaac was a pest and kept saying to Ishmael, "Wait for me, wait for me." And probably Ishmael said, "Oh go away, you're a spoiled brat and a baby."

Anyway, whatever the reason, Sarah grew more and more jealous and cross, and finally went to Abraham and said:

"I'm tired of my maid, and her son is mean to Isaac, so will you please get rid of them both? They can go back to Egypt for all I care, as long as they go."

Abraham was a bit upset because he liked Ishmael a lot and thought he was a splendid boy. But God said to Abraham, "Don't worry about it. Do what Sarah says. I'll look after Hagar and Ishmael."

So, early the next morning, Abraham took a bottle of water (only in those days they weren't bottles of glass or plastic, they were made of goatskin and goodness only knows what the water must have tasted like after a while, but you get used to anything, particularly if you are thirsty) and some bread and gave them to Hagar and told her to go away with Ishmael.

And Hagar and Ishmael wandered off rather vaguely into the desert, going aimlessly on until all their water was gone. Hagar was in despair and put Ishmael to sleep under a bush and walked away about the distance of a bowshot because she couldn't bear to see her son die from thirst. And she was crying and crying like anything.

Suddenly she heard an angel saying to her, "What *are* you crying for, Hagar? Why don't you use your eyes before you start crying, and look at what's right beside you? And don't you know that God is looking after you? Don't give up so easily. God is going to make a nation out of Ishmael as well as one out of Isaac, you know."

So Hagar dried her eyes and looked. And there, sure enough, was a well right by her, which she'd never noticed. She gave Ishmael a good drink and filled up the bottle, and on they went. Eventually they found some friends and must have managed all right because Ishmael grew up and had an Egyptian wife, and started a tribe called, rather understandably, the Ishmaelites.

Abraham and Isaac

ne day God decided to test Abraham. So He said, "Abraham."

And Abraham said, "Yes, I'm here."

Then God said, "Oh good. Well I'd like you to take your son, Isaac, whom you love so much, and go into the land of Moriah to a mountain I'll tell you about later, and there I'd like you to build an altar and sacrifice Isaac to me."

Now, though it may seem to be a pointless thing to us, quite a lot of the other desert wanderers in Abraham's time killed specially chosen people when they prayed to their gods. They thought it pleased their gods. In Abraham's camp they used animals — mostly baby goats and lambs — but Abraham would certainly have known about the custom of using people. So, though he was deeply distressed at God's request because he loved Isaac, he was not as horrified as we would be. He was just very sad that God wanted him to sacrifice his favorite person. It never occurred to him to say no, or to argue.

Early next morning Abraham woke up two of the young men in his camp and told them to get the donkey saddled, and woke up Isaac and told him to chop wood for the burnt offering they were going to make for God. They must have taken some provisions, too, because they walked for three days. They also carried fire with them, because there were no matches in those days.

After three days Abraham told the young men to wait with the donkey.

"The lad and I will go up this mountain to pray and then come back," he said.

He made Isaac carry the wood for the fire while he, Abraham, carried the fire and the knife for killing the burnt offering, and off they went up the mountain.

As they climbed, Isaac grew more and more mystified. He had often gone on these burnt-offering trips with Abraham, and he knew all about them. At last he simply could not contain his curiosity one minute longer and said, "Father?"

And Abraham said, "Here I am, my son."

"Well," said Isaac, "I can see the wood and the fire and the knife and all the usual paraphernalia we need for a burnt offering, but I can't see the lamb to use for the offering. Did you forget it?"

And Abraham said rather sternly, because he was sad, "My son, God will provide a lamb for the sacrifice Himself." So Isaac never said another word but walked on with Abraham.

At last they came to the place God had mentioned, and Abraham built the altar, piled the wood on it, tied up Isaac, put him on top of the wood and took out his big, sharp knife. Isaac knew now why they had no lamb with them.

Just as Abraham stretched out his hand with the knife, an angel called down from heaven:

"Stop! Don't kill Isaac. God does not want any human sacrifices at all. He just wanted to be sure you really would obey Him, even if it meant killing your only son."

Isaac must have been just as relieved about the change of plan as Abraham was, and when they looked about them they saw that a ram had very conveniently got himself caught by his horns in a thicket. So they used the ram instead.

And because God was pleased with Abraham, He renewed His promise about Abraham's descendants.

"They shall be as many as the stars in the sky and the sand upon the shore," said God.

Which is a great many.

Isaac and Rebekah

t about this time, Sarah died and Abraham bought a cave from a neighboring tribe to bury her in. He realized he was growing old too.

"Dear me," he thought. "I had better see about a wife for Isaac before I die too. He is quite old enough to get married."

So he called to him his chief servant who was in charge of the whole camp and all the camels, sheep, goats, donkeys and all that went on.

"Isaac needs a wife," said Abraham. "Will you please go back to the land I came from and get the family of my brother, Nahor, to help you pick a good wife for him?"

"Well, good gracious," said the servant, "shouldn't I take Isaac with me?"

"Oh no," said Abraham. "Just take some camels to my brother for a present."

So the servant set off with ten camels, while Isaac stayed behind without a murmur, waiting to see the wife he'd get.

When the servant came to Nahor's city in Mesopotamia, he went straight to the well to see what gossip he could collect. Everyone came to the well in the evenings to water the flocks and get water for themselves too. So there was always a lot of talk back and forth, and the servant sat down to wait, feeling quite nervous about the job he had to do.

"Perhaps I'll just pray to Abraham's God," he thought. "Please, God, could you help me in this tricky affair? Could you make it so that the first girl to offer me some water, and some to my camels too, shall be the right girl for Isaac?"

Scarcely had he finished praying when along came a most ravishingly beautiful girl who said, "Would you like a drink of water, and shall I get some for your camels?"

"Oh yes, please, how kind," said the servant, and when the camels had finished drinking, the servant gave the girl two gold bracelets and one gold earring, saying, "Who are you, by the way, and is there room in your house for me and my camels to stay?"

"Oh yes," answered the beautiful maiden. "There's heaps of room and straw in our house. Do come. I am Rebekah, the granddaughter of Nahor."

Nahor! Abraham's brother! What a bit of luck.

"Thank you, God," said the servant to himself. "She belongs to my master's family. I must be on the right track."

Rebekah ran home and told her brother, Laban, the story. Laban went to welcome the servant and ask him to dinner. But the servant refused to eat until he had told his story. He told how Abraham had prospered and had lots of gold and silver and servants and camels and goats and donkeys and sheep. He told how Abraham had sent him to find a wife for his only son. He told how he had prayed to God at the well and how everything seemed to be happening in exactly the right way.

In the end he said, "So now, tell me, what do you think? Do you agree?"

Then Rebekah's family said, "Yes. It seems as if the whole thing has been arranged by God. Take Rebekah to be Isaac's wife."

They did not bother to consult Rebekah because in those days the parents picked husbands and wives for their children, without any argument, and it seemed to work pretty well.

So Abraham's servant gave Rebekah some more gold and silver jewels and clothes, which he'd brought in case. And he gave Nahor the camels and had dinner and stayed the night.

Next morning he said to them, "Well, now I must be getting back to my master. He will be anxious to know how I have got on."

But they said to him, "Oh won't you stay for a week or ten days? Rebekah probably isn't ready yet."

Rebekah, however, was perfectly ready, so they said goodbye and set off. Rebekah took several of the servants — she called them handmaidens — and her nurse with her.

Meanwhile, back at the camp, Isaac was getting more and more nervous, hoping he'd like the wife he was brought because he would certainly be stuck with her whatever she was like. He went out every evening to scan the horizon for the dust that would mean the servant was returning.

At last, one evening, when he could bear the suspense no longer, he went out, and there were the camels in the distance! Isaac hurried out to greet them, and Rebekah saw him coming and said to the servant, "Who is that man rushing over toward us?"

"That's my master's son," the servant answered.

So Rebekah got off her camel and went to meet Isaac.

"Oh goodness, isn't he handsome," she thought.

"Oh goodness, isn't she beautiful," thought Isaac.

And luckily they fell in love and were married and began to live happily ever after.

Abraham was delighted with the way everything had come to pass, and he died very peacefully at a ripe old age. Isaac buried him in the cave with Sarah, and Ishmael came to the funeral. Goodness only knows how he knew about it.

Esau and Jacob

After a while, Isaac and Rebekah had twin sons, called Esau and Jacob. They were not at all alike as some twins are but were totally different as many twins are. The elder one was Esau, and he was big and strong and hairy and loved to go hunting. Jacob, the younger twin, was smooth and not so energetic and preferred sitting around in the tents, thinking. So instead of liking them both the same, Isaac preferred Esau because he hunted delicious venison for him, and Rebekah preferred Jacob because he hung about the place and kept her company. Naturally this led to trouble in the end.

When Isaac was old and his eyes were dim so that he could not see, he realized he might soon die. So he sent for Esau and said, "I'm getting rather old now and might die any day. So will you please take your bow and arrow, hunt some venison and get your mother to make one of those delicious pies that I love. Then I'll eat it and give you my blessing so that I'll be ready to die."

In those days, if they thought they were dying, they had a custom of giving a special blessing to the son they liked best. This blessing would make that son the boss of the whole camp and owner of all the camels, goats, donkeys, slaves, gold and silver, and jewels, and everyone would have to obey him. This was the blessing Isaac planned for Esau.

Now, unbeknownst to Isaac, Rebekah had been listening and she, of course, wanted Jacob to get that blessing and be top man. So she thought of a cheating plot. She called Jacob to her and said, "Quickly go and get me a couple of kids and I'll make your father some stew. Then you can take it to him and get Esau's blessing."

Here you would expect Jacob to say, "Oh but mother, that would be cheating and very, very wrong."

But did he? Dear me, no, not on your life. He said, "Oh yes, what a good idea. But my brother is a hairy man and I am a smooth one. Peradventure my father will touch me, and when he finds out it's me, he'll curse me, not bless me."

"Oh good heavens," said Rebekah impatiently, "I've thought about that, naturally. Just hurry up and get those kids or it will be too late."

Perhaps it should be mentioned here that kids means baby goats, not children.

So Jacob got the kids, and Rebekah made them into a succulent stew and then set about disguising Jacob as Esau. She put Esau's clothes on him to make him smell right and tied goatskins on his arms to make him feel right. Then she gave him the stew and said, "There you are. Now hurry, before Esau gets back and ruins it all."

Quickly Jacob went into Isaac's tent and said:

"Hello, father. I've brought you your venison pie and I'm all ready for the blessing."

"Well, that was very quick," said Isaac. "How did you do it so quickly?"

"Oh, God helped me," lied Jacob.

Then Isaac said, "Come here, my son, so that I can feel you and be sure you really are Esau. I am very blind these days."

So Isaac felt Jacob's arms with the goatskin on and smelled the smell of the outdoors on Esau's clothes, and said, "Well, your voice sounds like Jacob's, but you feel and smell like Esau, so give me the stew and I'll eat it and then I'll bless you."

With a sigh of relief Jacob gave him the stew. Isaac ate it and gave Jacob the blessing.

"God shall bless you with lots of corn and wine. Anyone who curses you shall be cursed, anyone who blesses you shall be blessed. Everyone shall bow down before you and do as you tell them."

As soon as he'd finished, Jacob left the tent. And not a moment too soon either, because in came Esau, feeling very cheerful.

"Hello father," he said. "I'm back with your stew, so won't you eat it and bless me?"

"Wh . . . wh . . . who are you?" asked Isaac in a funny voice.

"Why I'm Esau, of course. Whoever else?" answered Esau in amazement.

Isaac trembled with the shock and said, "Esau? Esau? Then who was it who just came in with some stew and got the blessing? Whoever it was, it's too late now; he can't be unblessed. It must have been Jacob after all. I *thought* it didn't sound like you."

"You mean there's no blessing left for me?" asked Esau.

"No," said Isaac. "I've given the main blessing. I can give you only a very minor one, I'm afraid."

So Esau got a very small blessing and burst out of Isaac's tent in a towering rage.

"Where's Jacob?" he shouted. "Where's that hateful, loathsome, cheating brother of mine? Just wait until I find him. I'll break every bone in his body, the mean, under-handed wretch. I'll hit him, I'll beat him, I'll kill him, just see if I don't!"

Rebekah heard him storming about and said to Jacob, "Look, your brother's in a bit of a temper with you. You'd better go to my brother Laban for a while until Esau cools down. While you're there, you might find a decent wife for yourself. I don't want you marrying any of those tiresome Ishmaelites as Esau has."

So Jacob hurried off to the land where Laban lived, and Esau couldn't find him. Instead, Esau annoyed his mother by marrying another Ishmaelite. You see, it was perfectly customary in those days to have two or three wives at once. Having one at a time is quite a modern idea.

Jacob and Rachel

J acob, meanwhile, set out for Haran, where Laban lived. It was quite a long way and Jacob was walking, so when night came Jacob made a pile of stone for his pillow and lay down on the hard ground to sleep. And while he was asleep he had a very vivid dream. He dreamed there was a ladder on the ground that was so tall it reached all the way up to heaven, and there were angels going up on it and coming down on it. At the very top of the ladder Jacob dreamed he saw God.

And God said to him, "I am the God of Abraham and of Isaac. All this land to the north, to the south, to the east and west, I will give to your family and their descendants. All the families on the earth shall be blessed because of you and your family. And I shall be with you, and will stay with you and help you. I won't leave you until I've done what I've just promised."

Then Jacob woke up and was terrified.

"Oh, goodness," he said. "This must be the house of God and the gate of heaven, and I never knew it."

So he got up and took his stone pillow and made a pillar of it and made a return promise to God, saying, "If God will really be with me and look after me and help me get food to eat and clothes to wear, and will bring me safely back home, then He shall be my God, too, as well as Abraham's and Isaac's. And of everything that God gives me, I shall give him back a tenth."

Then Jacob journeyed on, and after many days he came to Haran, and as everyone did, he headed straight for the well in the evening. This well had a very heavy stone lid on it, so when a beautiful girl brought some sheep for a drink, Jacob helped her and asked her who she was.

"My name is Rachel," she said. "I'm the daughter of Laban."

"Oh are you?" said Jacob. "How simply delightful. My mother is Laban's sister!"

"Gracious me," said Rachel. "That makes us cousins! I must rush and tell my father. He'll be so pleased."

So Rachel ran to tell Laban, and Laban ran back to kiss Jacob and invite him to stay. Jacob made himself so useful and worked so hard with the flocks that after a while Laban said, "Just because you're my nephew doesn't mean you have to work for nothing. What would you like me to pay you?"

"Oh, how kind of you," answered Jacob. "But what I'd really like best would be if instead of wages, I could marry

Rachel, because I really love her so much that I desperately want to marry her."

Laban said, "All right. If you work for me for seven years, you can marry Rachel."

And Jacob loved Rachel so much that the seven years seemed but a day. At the end of the seven years Jacob said to Laban, "I've worked for seven years. Can I marry Rachel now, please?"

So Laban gathered everyone together and made a huge wedding feast, and everyone had a gay time; the bride was brought in completely hidden by her veil, and Jacob married her.

Then Jacob took off his wife's veil and, oh dear me! It was not Rachel at all! It was her older sister, Leah, who had very pretty eyes but was not nearly as beautiful as Rachel, and Jacob didn't love her at all. He was very upset.

"What's the idea of this?" he said. "It's Rachel I want, not Leah. This is quite the wrong one."

"Oh yes, I know," said Laban, "but we have a custom here that the older one has to be married first, before the younger one can get married. But don't worry. You can marry Rachel next week if you like, and work another seven years."

So Jacob married Rachel a week later and worked for Laban for another seven years. Then God told Jacob it was time for him to take his wives and flocks and household back to Canaan.

"All the land that I gave to Abraham and Isaac I will give to you, and I won't call you Jacob anymore. I shall call you Israel."

So Jacob and his belongings set off for Canaan, although Laban was none too pleased about it.

On their way they met Esau, who had quite recovered his temper and even refused a present of sheep Jacob offered him. He said he had enough of his own.

Soon after Jacob's return, Isaac died, and Jacob and Esau buried him.

Joseph and His Brethren

As the years passed, Rachel became very unhappy because Leah had children and she had none. Leah had ten sons, called Reuben, Simeon, Levi, Judah, Issachar, Zebulon, Dan, Naphtali, Gad and Asher. Actually, they weren't all Leah's sons. Some of them belonged to her hand maiden. In those days, if you had handmaidens, they often had children for you.

Since Jacob still loved Rachel the best, he was unhappy, too, that she had no children. So you can imagine how happy they were when, after many, many years, Rachel at long last had a son. They called him Joseph, and Jacob adored him and spoiled him. He spoiled him so much that his ten older brothers hated him and never said a kind word to him. Even when Rachel had a second son, called Benjamin, Jacob still liked Joseph best and spoiled him the most. He gave him a coat of many colors, which made the brothers even more jealous.

Joseph didn't care. In fact, he often said annoying things to his brothers on purpose. He used to dream particularly irritating dreams and tell them to his brethren.

One day he said to them, "Guess what I dreamed last night? I dreamed we were all tying up our bundles of wheat in the field, and *my* bundle stood up, and all *your* bundles came and bowed down to it."

His brothers were enraged.

"You conceited little thing," they said. "Do you really think great strong men like us are going to bow down to a spoiled brat like you?"

And they hated him even more.

Soon he had another dream, which he hastened to tell them.

"Just listen to this dream then," he said. "I dreamed that the sun and moon and eleven stars came and bowed down to me."

This time his father was listening, and even he thought it was going a bit too far. He said, "What's all this? Do you really think your mother and I and your brethren will bow down to you? No, no. That is overdoing it."

So his brethren were jealous and crossly took the sheep a long way away to Shechem, to find fresh grass.

After a few weeks Jacob wanted to know how the flocks were doing, so he said to Joseph, "Would you go over to Shechem, please, to find out how your brethren are, and then come back and tell me?"

Joseph said, "Certainly. I'll go at once."

When he got to Shechem, however, Joseph found no sign of his brethren or the flocks. While he was wandering around looking lost, a man said to him, "Hello, boy. Are you looking for something?"

"Oh yes," said Joseph. "I thought my ten brethren and hundreds of sheep were here."

"Oh them," said the man. "Yes, they were here, but they've gone now. I heard them say, 'Let's go to Dothan.' Why don't you try Dothan?"

"Thank you very much," said Joseph. "I will."

So Joseph went on to Dothan; but long before he arrived, his brethren saw him coming and made a plot to get rid of him.

"Look," said one brother, "here comes that dastardly dreamer. Why don't we kill him and put him in this pit and say some evil beast has devoured him? Then we'll see what comes of his idiotic dreams."

Most of the brethren agreed to this. But Reuben, who was slightly kinder and the eldest, said, "I don't think we ought to kill him because that would be murder, and murder isn't the right thing. Why don't we just put him in the pit and leave him there?"

Reuben really meant to rescue Joseph later and give him back to Jacob, but the brethren didn't realize this and agreed not to murder him. So Reuben went off to see to the flocks and Joseph arrived. Instantly the brethren stripped off his coat of many colors and cast him into the pit without even any water. While they sat close by eating their picnic lunch, along came some Ishmaelite traders on their way to Egypt. Judah had a brain wave.

"I say," he said to the brethren. "Why don't we sell Joseph to these traders? That way no one could accuse us of being murderers."

So Joseph was hauled up out of the pit and sold to the Ishmaelites for twenty pieces of silver. And the traders took him to Egypt.

When Reuben returned and found that Joseph had disappeared, he was distraught.

"What shall I do?" he asked. "Where is the boy? Oh dear. Oh dear, whatever shall we say to Jacob?"

But the other brothers were very glad.

"Don't be so silly, Reuben," they said. "Joseph was a pain. It's lovely to be rid of him. We're dipping his coat in goat's blood to show our father when we get back."

And they brought the coat to Jacob and said, "Look what we found on the way. Do you think it is Joseph's coat of many colors by any chance?"

And Jacob said, "Yes, it is my son's coat. An evil beast must have devoured him. Joseph is, without doubt, rent in pieces."

Jacob was heartbroken, and wore sackcloth and ashes for a long, long time. In those days they always wore sackcloth and ashes when they were unhappy. But the brethren were happy.

Meanwhile, in Egypt, Joseph had been sold to a man called Potiphar, who was a guard for the Egyptian pharaoh, which is what the Egyptians called their king.

Joseph in Prison

Joseph worked hard for Potiphar for many years, and because he was excellent at arranging things, Potiphar put him in charge of his whole household. Joseph remembered about Jacob's God and always prayed to him and not to Pharaoh the way the Egyptians did. Without his ten brethren around to be jealous of him, Joseph stopped being a spoiled brat and grew up wise and clever.

Unfortunately, Potiphar had a most tiresomely interfering wife who told Potiphar a whole parcel of lies about Joseph and accused him of things he had never done. But Potiphar believed her, because if you don't believe your wife, life gets most awkward. So Joseph was put in prison without a trial.

Before very long, the prison keeper found out how good Joseph was at things and put him in charge of the other prisoners. Joseph became especially friendly with Pharaoh's butler and baker, who were also in prison. One morning, on his rounds, Joseph found the butler and baker looking thoroughly glum.

"Well, good morning you two," said Joseph. "You look thoroughly dismal and gloomy this morning. What's the matter with you?"

So they said to Joseph, "Oh dear, we've both had simply fascinating dreams, but there aren't any dream interpreters in this prison, so we don't know what our dreams mean."

And Joseph said, "Well goodness me, if that's all that's bothering you, I can probably tell you what your dreams mean. God tells me the meanings, you know."

"Oh, does He?" said the butler. "How perfectly splendid. Here's my dream, then. I dreamed I had three vines in my hand. Then the grapes appeared and I squeezed them into Pharaoh's cup and gave the cup to Pharaoh. What does that mean?"

"That's simple," said Joseph. "The three vines are three days, and it means that in three days Pharoah will send for you to go back and be his butler. So when you're back at work, will you please remember about me and tell Pharaoh I have done nothing to deserve being put in this dungeon?"

"Oh yes, certainly," said the butler, feeling most happy about his dream.

Then the baker told Joseph his dream.

"I dreamed I had three baskets on my head full of cakes for Pharaoh, but the birds came and ate them all up. What does that mean?"

"Well," said Joseph, "I'm afraid that's not quite so jolly. The three baskets mean three days, too, but in three days Pharaoh will decide to chop off your head and the vultures will eat you up."

And Joseph was right. Three days later it was Pharaoh's birthday, and he sent for his butler out of jail to organize the feast. But he decided the baker bored him and ordered his head to be chopped off. Poor baker, but no one dared to disobey Pharaoh. And anyway, for all we know he really might have done something wicked.

But do you think the butler remembered Joseph left languishing in prison? No, he did not. He ungratefully forgot all about him until one morning two whole years later.

Joseph and Pharoah

ne morning two years later when the butler took Pharaoh his breakfast wine, he noticed that Pharaoh looked very worried.

"Good morning, Pharaoh," said the butler. "You look rather upset this morning. Is there something bothering you?"

"Well, yes, as a matter of fact, there is," answered Pharaoh. "You see, I had some rather long and interesting dreams the other day, but not one of my magicians could tell me what on earth they mean."

"Oh, my goodness," said the butler guiltily. "I had entirely forgotten; but when I was in prison with the baker, there was a young Hebrew there who was marvelous at explaining dreams, and he explained ours to us. Why don't you see if he can help you?"

Pharaoh said, "Send for him immediately."

So people rushed off to the dungeon and got Joseph washed and shaved and into some clean clothes, and brought him to Pharaoh.

And Pharaoh said, "Good morning. I've had some rather unusual dreams that no one can explain, and I gather you're good at this kind of thing?"

"Well, it isn't me, you know," said Joseph. "It's God. He tells me the meaning."

"I see," said Pharaoh. "Well, I dreamed that seven sleek, well-fed cows came up out of the river and fed in a meadow. Then seven wretched, half-starved cows such as I never saw in all Egypt came out of the river too. And the seven wretched cows ate up the seven fat cows, but when they'd finished they were just as thin as ever. Then I woke up. After I went to sleep again I had another dream about seven good fat ears of corn being devoured by seven withered, blasted ears of corn. I told all this to my magicians, but they didn't seem to understand. What do you make of it?"

"God has told me the answer," said Joseph. "Both dreams mean the same thing, and you've had them twice over to make sure you get the message. It means that there are going to be seven years of plenty, with excellent harvests and plenty of food, and then there will be seven years of rotten harvest and starvation and famine. It will be very grievous."

"Oh dear," said Pharaoh. "How perfectly ghastly. Whatever shall I do about it? What a dreadful worry."

"Well, if I were you," said Joseph sensibly, "I'd look for a wise and honest man, and get him to organize barn building throughout Egypt. During the seven plentiful years the barns can be filled with spare corn and food. Then it can all be sold off gradually during the seven lean years."

"Oh, yes, of course," said Pharaoh. "What a good idea. Well, since you are obviously wise and rather bossy, you can be the man."

Then Pharaoh took off his ring and gave it to Joseph, saying, "Here is my ring. You shall be the grandest man in the whole of Egypt except me, and everyone must bow to you. You shall have expensive clothes and a gold chain around your neck, and your chariot shall go behind mine, and I'll give you a wife as well."

"Oh thank you very much," said Joseph.

So what a change for Joseph! From prison to palace in a twinkling. What would have happened if Joseph had been wrong about the dreams, we can only conjecture. Fortunately for him, it all came about as he had predicted. For seven years the harvests were superabundant, and Joseph went all over Egypt getting barns built and filling them with spare food. He also had two sons, called Ephraim and Manasseh.

Then the seven years of plenty ended and the seven years of dearth began, and Joseph opened up the storehouses. Everyone came to Joseph to buy corn, and he was very fair and honest about the whole thing.

Joseph and His Brethren Again

radually the famine spread far beyond Egypt until it reached the land of Canaan, where Joseph's brothers were, and his father, Jacob, now an old man.

Joseph's ten elder brothers never really had much sense or initiative. Maybe that was the real reason they were so jealous of Joseph, who had lots of both. Be that as it may, when they began to starve, they couldn't think what to do about it, until eventually the aged Jacob grew impatient.

"Why do you sit about looking at each other and moaning?" he said. "*Do* something. Haven't you heard that there's plenty of food in Egypt? Go and buy some, for goodness sake, before we all starve."

"Yes, Father," they said, "all right."

So Joseph's ten brethren went off to Egypt to buy corn. But Jacob kept Benjamin, Joseph's youngest brother, at home.

"Lest peradventure mischief befall him," he said. "I don't want to risk losing Benjamin as well as Joseph."

After a long, tiring and, presumably, hungry journey, the ten brethren arrived in Egypt and went to the governor of the land to see about buying corn. When they saw the governor, they didn't know it was Joseph. For one thing he was dressed like an Egyptian prince, for another he spoke Egyptian, and anyway Joseph was the last person they were expecting to meet ever again. So, of course, because he was obviously a very mighty prince, the brethren bowed down to him exactly as his dreams had so annoyingly foretold.

Joseph recognized his brothers at once, however, because they had merely grown older. But he decided to test them to see if they'd grown nicer as well.

"Good morning," he said very haughtily. "And where, pray, have you come from?"

And they said, "We've come from Canaan to buy food, because of the famine."

"Fiddlesticks and nonsense," said Joseph. "You're quite obviously spies."

"Oh no, my lord, we really aren't," said the brethren earnestly. "We're all brothers and we've only come to buy corn."

"I don't believe a word of it," said Joseph. "You're spies, I say. You look just like spies to me. You've come to see how much food we've got here."

The brethren began to get really worried now and started telling him the story of their lives.

"We are twelve sons of one man," they said. "Our youngest brother is at home with our father, and one brother is no more."

"It sounds like a taradiddle of nonsense to me," said Joseph. "If it's the truth, then one of you must go and get your youngest brother, while I clap the rest of you in jail. Otherwise, I'll go instantly and tell Pharaoh you're spies."

So he put them all in prison for three days to worry, and then went to them and said, "I have decided to be kind and let you all go except one. The rest of you can take the corn home and come back with your youngest brother."

"Oh dear," said the brethren to each other in their own language, "this must be punishment for what we did to Joseph all those years ago."

And Reuben said, "Didn't I *tell* you we shouldn't hurt Joseph? Now look what's come of it. You wouldn't listen to me."

Little did they suspect that Joseph understood everything they were saying! But he said nothing, because he wanted to see how much they cared about hurting Jacob any more. So he tied up Simeon and put him back in prison while the rest went home, quite unaware that Joseph had ordered his steward to put their money back into their sacks with the corn.

"Hello," said Jacob when they got back. "Where's Simeon?"

They had to tell him the whole ghastly story of Joseph keeping Simeon until they took Benjamin to prove they weren't spies.

"Well, I'm sorry for Simeon," said Jacob, "but you're not taking Benjamin."

When the brethren opened up their sacks of corn to cook a decent meal, they found their money had been given back to them, and they were all afraid. Jacob was very much upset.

"Really, this is too much," he said. "Joseph is no more. Simeon is as good as dead. You want to take Benjamin away, and on top of it all, you can't even manage to pay for the corn when you buy it. What a hopeless lot of incompetents you are."

Reuben said to him, "Look, I swear I'll guard Benjamin with my life, and if anything happens to him, you can slay my two sons."

"Benjamin's not going and that's all there is to it," said Jacob. "If anything happens to him, you'll bring down my gray hairs with sorrow to the grave, and slaying your sons wouldn't bring back Benjamin anyway."

So life returned to its normal routine, except, presumably, for Simeon's wife and children. But the brethren did not know — as we do and as Joseph did — that the next six harvests were going to be rotten too, and that they would be compelled once again to face a trudge to Egypt.

A year later starvation and famine once more stalked the land, and Jacob told the brethren to go to Egypt again. But Judah said, "We'll only go if Benjamin comes, too. That man in Egypt will put us all in prison if we don't bring Benjamin, and we might just as well starve here as rot in some foreign dungeon."

And Jacob said, "Oh for heavens sake. *Why* did you have to tell him about Benjamin?"

The brethren said, "Well, he asked us most particularly, 'Have you a father? Have you another brother?' so naturally we told him. Could we have known he'd be so odd as to want to see him? If we don't take Benjamin and go soon for corn, we will all starve. Our wives will starve, our children will starve, our camels will starve, our donkeys will starve, and then where will we be?"

At last Judah said to Jacob, "Look here, father. We've got to do something. Send the lad with me. I promise I won't let him out of my sight, and if I don't bring him safely back, I will take the blame forever."

In those days they were much more honorable about keeping promises than people are nowadays, and if they broke a promise, they were apt to feel guilty and wretched for the rest of their lives. So at last Jacob gave in, as there really was no alternative but starvation.

"Oh all right," he said unwillingly. "But take some honey and nuts and spices as a present for the man, and take double money too. Peradventure it was an oversight that your money was put back into your sacks."

So the brethren set out once more for Egypt. And Benjamin went, too, leaving Jacob bereft of all his sons. Poor Jacob! He certainly had been made to pay for having cheated Esau of the blessing!

Joseph and Benjamin

J oseph saw his brethren coming and saw that Benjamin was with them. He ordered his steward to bring them all to his house. The brethren were terrified that it was because of the money they had found in their sacks, and nervously explained to the steward that they'd brought double money this time.

"Oh, that's all right," said the steward, "don't worry about that. Your God must have put money in your sacks. We didn't. We had your money."

So they were brought to Joseph's house and given water to wash their feet. People were always offered water to wash their feet when they went visiting, because of all the sand and dust. Then Simeon was brought out, and they all waited in suspense until noon, when Joseph came. They gave Joseph his present and bowed some more.

"Ah, thank you, how kind," said Joseph. "And how is your father, is he still alive and well?"

"Yes, indeed," said the brethren. "Our father is in excellent health." And they bowed again.

Then Joseph looked at Benjamin and said, "And is this the youngest brother of whom you spoke?"

"Yes," said Benjamin. "I'm Benjamin."

Joseph was so overcome by the immense joy of seeing his youngest brother, whom he loved and had missed, that he had to go to his room for a short while to weep with happiness. Then he felt better, washed his face and went back out, and said, "Well, now, how about some lunch?"

So they all went to lunch with Joseph and were amazed to find that they'd been arranged according to age.

"How peculiar," said one brother. "Look, we're all in our right ages."

"Good gracious, so we are," said another. "And look, Benjamin keeps getting five times as much food as we do. I must say, this grand Egyptian does have some remarkably strange notions."

Of course, they still had no idea that Joseph understood their every word. He always used an interpreter to talk to them so that they would suspect nothing.

After lunch, Joseph again gave secret orders to his steward.

"Go and put their money back in their sacks," he said, "and in Benjamin's sack, put my favorite silver mug as well."

The steward was slightly startled.

"You mean you're going to give away your best silver mug?" he asked.

"No, not precisely," said Joseph. "Just go and do it anyway."

So it was done, and the unsuspecting brethren left. No sooner had they got outside the city than Joseph sent for his steward again and said, "Go and chase after those men, and when you overtake them, say to them, 'Why have you returned evil for good? My master says you are thieves and have stolen his most valued silver mug.'"

So the steward, feeling thoroughly perplexed, went out to collect some guards.

"Goodness knows what peculiar game my master is up to now," he thought. "I can't make it out at all. First it's 'Give them my mug,' then it's 'Go and call them thieves.' The whole thing sounds crazy to me."

But off he went to overtake the brethren as instructed, and to say what he had been told to say.

"Thieves?" said the brethren. "Us? Oh no. We assure you, you're mistaken. We have nothing but gratitude for your master. Why should we steal any of his gold or silver?"

"Well anyway, we have got to search your sacks to see," said the steward.

"Oh please do," said the brothers, knowing their innocence. "And if you find the mug in anyone's sack, then you can take that one to be your master's slave."

So the steward searched the sacks, starting with the oldest brother's and ending with Benjamin's, and in Benjamin's, of course, they found the mug.

The brethren were horror-stricken.

"There must be some ghastly mistake," they said. "We must all go back with Benjamin."

And in terror and consternation, they all returned and bowed down to Joseph.

"God is punishing us for our sins," they said. "We are all your servants, we *and* Benjamin."

"Oh that's all right," said Joseph. "You needn't all stay. I'll just keep Benjamin. The rest of you can go back to your father in peace."

He did not mean it, of course. He was still testing them to see if they cared about making Jacob unhappy. So now Judah was in a quandary because of the promise he had made to Jacob. He said:

"Please, sir, don't be vexed if I say something, but do you remember the first time we came, how you asked us about our father and whether we had any other brothers, and we explained that one brother was no more and one was still at home because our father loved him most now?"

"Yes," said Joseph. "I do remember, and I said you were to bring him to me to prove you weren't spies, so you did, and he's a thief, so I shall make him my slave."

Poor Judah became desperate.

"Oh no, no, indeed we cannot let that happen," he said. "If we go back without Benjamin, our father will die of sorrow because he is old and has been unhappy ever since our other brother went away. I could not do that to him.

Please, let Benjamin go back to our father and keep me instead. I am strong and will work hard, I promise. Or keep *all* of us. *Any*thing, but keep Benjamin. We truly couldn't do such a thing to our old father."

By now Joseph knew that his brethren had grown much nicer, and he could bear the suspense no longer. He sent all the Egyptians out of the room and wept out loud. The Egyptians in his house all heard and wondered whatever was going on.

"I am Joseph," he said to his brethren in their own language. "I am Joseph. Is my father really alive?"

The brethren were speechless with amazement, so Joseph went on. "I am your brother Joseph, whom you sold all those years ago. But don't be angry with yourselves for doing it, because God arranged it all so that I could come here and save your lives in this famine. There are still five more hopeless harvests to come, and God needed me here to be a ruler throughout Egypt to save people's lives and yours too. Look, it really and truly is me!"

And he kissed them all, especially Benjamin, and they finally found their tongues and began talking. Soon everyone knew what had happened. Pharaoh was most amused by the entire thing and gave them camels and chariots and endless presents, and commanded them to go and fetch their father and their families and to come back and live in Egypt.

So the brethren all went back to Jacob and said to him, "Guess what! You'll never believe it, but the governor of all Egypt is actually our long-lost brother, Joseph!"

Jacob was tremendously surprised. In fact, he fainted. But when he revived and saw all the presents, he believed them and said, "It is enough. My son Joseph is yet alive. I will go and see him before I die."

So they packed up all their belongings and went to Egypt. And Joseph went to meet his father and take them all to see Pharaoh. Pharaoh was delighted to see them and asked them what they liked doing best.

"Oh, we like looking after cattle best," they said. Joseph had warned them not to say they were shepherds, because for some reason the Egyptians didn't care for shepherds.

"Good, that's splendid," said Pharaoh. "You can live in part of Egypt called Goshen and look after all my cattle for me."

As this was precisely what Joseph had wanted Pharaoh to say, everyone was delighted, and Jacob and his whole tribe lived in Goshen from then on, looking after Pharaoh's cattle. And the tribe grew and multiplied exceedingly. Here, Jacob began to be called Israel, the name God had given him all those years ago when he first left Laban. So his sons and grandsons began to be called the Children of Israel, regardless of age.

Seventeen years later, Jacob died, and Joseph and his brethren buried him in Mamre, in Abraham's cave.

Miriam and Moses

For many hundreds of years, the Children of Israel went on living in Goshen, and there were many thousands of them. Pharaohs came and went, until there came one of a nervous and nasty disposition. He was nervous, because he began worrying that there might be too many Children of Israel, and they might decide to fight the Egyptians. He was nasty because he thought he could solve the problem by making the Israelites into slaves. He never stopped to remember that without Joseph, there would not have been any Egyptians worth bothering about.

So the Israelites were made to work, building cities and pyramids and making bricks for the Egyptians. And cruel Egyptian taskmasters stood over them, forcing them to work ever faster and harder. But it was all to no avail as far as the population was concerned. The Children of Israel went on having just as many babies as ever, and their population grew larger and larger.

So Pharaoh called his ministers together again and said, "This won't do. We shall soon be completely overrun by Israelites, so I've hit upon the idea of throwing all their baby boys into the river Nile. How does that strike you?"

"Oh what a superb scheme," said the ministers.

Pharaoh hastened to implement his plan, and presumably the Nile crocodiles approved of this change in breakfast food. But the Israelites, rather naturally, were utterly opposed to the entire idea. One mother in particular, called Jochebed, determined to do something about it.

When Jochebed had a baby boy, she hid him in her house until he got too noisy to hide. Then she made a little basket for him out of bulrushes and painted it with pitch to make it seaworthy, then put the baby in it.

She called her daughter, Miriam, and said, "Listen carefully, Miriam. I'm going to put the baby in this basket and hide him in the irises at the edge of the river. I want you to hide close by to make sure nothing happens to him."

So Jochebed put the baby in the basket at the river's brink, and Miriam kept watch.

Before very long Pharaoh's daughter came walking along the river bank and decided to go into the river for an early morning swim. She had her maidens with her, and probably they woke the baby up with their chatter. He started to cry, and the princess saw the little basket. She sent one of her maidens paddling in to fetch it out. The maiden brought it to the princess, who opened it up. The baby yelled loudly.

"Well fancy that!" said the princess. "It must be one of the Hebrew babies. I think I shall adopt him. He looks so sweet, and it will give me something amusing to do. I shall have to find a nurse somewhere, of course."

Miriam, who had been watching in a dreadful state of nerves, instantly grasped her opportunity, darted rapidly out of hiding, and went up to the princess and curtsied.

"Please, miss," she said. "I couldn't help hearing what you said, and if it's a baby-sitter you want, I know a fearfully good one who wants a job."

"Oh, you do?" said the princess. "How handy. Go and send her to the palace."

"Oh yes, indeed. I certainly will," said Miriam gleefully, and she raced off home to tell her mother. Her mother went immediately to the palace to apply for the job of looking after her own son! A very crafty idea, indeed.

The princess called the baby Moses. We do not know whether Jochebed liked the name, but it undoubtedly was better than having her baby thrown nameless to the crocodiles.

Moses in Midian

The years passed by and Moses grew to be a man. But he was rather a cowardly man. This may have been because he was really very mixed up. Here he was, living like an Egyptian prince in laziness and luxury, while all the time he knew that he was really a Hebrew, because his nurse-mother must certainly have told him.

So it made him thoroughly uncomfortable whenever he saw the Egyptian taskmasters being cruel to the Israelites. But he never knew what to do about it, until one day he saw an Egyptian beating a Hebrew. Then Moses looked this way and that way, and when he saw there was no one looking, he slew the Egyptian and buried him in the sand.

Naturally the news leaked out, and Pharaoh was furious and ordered Moses to be killed. So Moses ran away. But the Hebrews didn't want him either, because they didn't trust him with his Egyptian upbringing. Poor Moses. He had to flee from everyone he knew to a faraway land called Midian.

When Moses reached Midian, he sat down at the well to rest, in the time-honored tradition. And, true to tradition, ere long there came to the well seven lovely maidens with their father's flocks to water.

Then some rough, rude shepherds came along and pushed the maidens aside.

"Out of the way, you girls," they said bossily. "We're getting our flocks watered first."

"Oh no, you're not," said Moses, springing into action. "Come here, lovely maidens. I will help you, and the shepherds can just wait."

Naturally the girls were delighted not to have to wait, and they got back home to their father, Jethro, much earlier than usual.

"Good heavens, you're home early today," said Jethro. "What happened?"

"Oh well," said the girls, "when we got to the well, there was a very handsome man there who helped us and made the shepherds wait."

"Oh I see," said Jethro. "And where is he now? Did you invite him to supper?"

"Oh dear, no, we didn't," said the maidens. "We never thought of it."

Jethro was exasperated. With seven daughters to marry off, where were their wits wandering to leave an eligible man sitting by the well?

"Well honestly," he said. "A lovely man helps you, and you don't even offer him a meal. Really I am ashamed of you. Go and fetch him at once."

So Moses was fetched, and Jethro invited him to stay and gave him one of his seven daughters, Zipporah, for a wife, and this left only six more husbands to find. Moses stayed there for quite a while, peacefully married and looking after Jethro's flocks.

One day God decided it was high time someone rescued the Children of Israel. He looked around for a suitable man for the job, and His eye alighted on Moses in Midian.

"Ah," said God to Himself. "Just the fellow I'm looking for. And he can speak Egyptian too, as well as Hebrew."

Moses and the Burning Bush

Unaware that his peaceful existence was so soon to be shattered, Moses continued looking after Jethro's sheep by day. In the evenings he took them back to wherever they were camped and spent quiet evenings with his wife and baby sons.

Until one day . . .

One day Moses led his flock of sheep around the edge of the desert near a mountain called Horeb. There was probably not a great deal of grass about, it being near the desert, but there were a few rather scrubby bushes growing, and Moses thought the sheep might find them tasty. To his utter amazement, as he looked at the bushes, one of them burst into flames. To his even greater astonishment, the bush was not burned up.

"Good gracious me," said Moses to himself and the sheep. "I had better go and see this great sight, and find out why the bush is on fire but not burning up."

So Moses went to inspect the bush.

"Well, that really is pretty odd. On fire but not burning. Most peculiar. What can it mean, I wonder?"

Then the bush spoke.

"Moses, Moses," said the bush.

"Oh ho, so you talk, too, do you," said Moses. "That means it must be God, so no wonder the bush isn't being burned up."

"Yes, that's right," said God. "Don't come any closer, and take off your shoes, too. This is holy ground."

"Oh, all right," said Moses. "And now what can I do for you?"

"I want you to go and rescue the Children of Israel for me," said God. "Pharaoh is being so dreadfully cruel to them that it's time they left Egypt. So perhaps you'll just set out at once and rescue them."

Moses was utterly appalled at the suggestion.

"Who, *me?*" he said. "Oh no, I couldn't possibly do that. I'm hopeless at that sort of thing. I simply can never think of a thing to say in public. I'd just bungle the entire affair. You'd really better think of someone else. It's simply not me at all."

"Nonsense," said God. "My mind is made up. You must go and lead my people into a land of milk and honey."

"But I don't know how," said poor Moses desperately. "Pharaoh doesn't like me, and he certainly won't say, 'Oh, yes, of course Moses dear, do take the Children of Israel anywhere you like,' and, anyway, even if he did, how do I know they'd come with me? And how do *I* know where this land flowing with milk and honey *is?* No, no, if you don't mind, I'd really *much* rather not take this job. I'm sure you could find someone else if you looked."

But God was adamant.

"For goodness sake stop making excuses, Moses," He said, "and *listen* to me. Go to the Children of Israel and say, 'The God of Abraham, Isaac and Jacob has sent me to rescue you,' and go to Pharaoh and tell him you've been talking to me and that I want you to take my people into the desert for three days to pray."

Moses was hating the whole idea more every minute, and getting more and more frightened.

"But they won't listen to me," he said. "They'll say, 'Oh rubbish, of course you haven't been talking to God — what a likely tale.'"

Then God said, "What's that in your hand?"

"This old thing, you mean?" asked Moses. "That's my rod for directing the sheep and pulling them up if they get stuck. In fact, it's my shepherd's crook."

"Well, throw it down on the ground," said God.

Moses threw it down and it turned into a serpent, and Moses ran away his fastest.

"Oh, do come back, do," said God. "Just pick it up by its tail. So Moses rather nervously picked it up by its tail, and it instantly turned back into his rod.

"There," said God. "If they don't believe your voice, they'll believe the sign. Now will you please do as I ask and go to Egypt?"

But Moses still said, "I really wish you'd send someone else."

Then God got cross and said, "Well I won't. I'm sending you. I've given you a sign to help you. I will even go with you to tell you what to say. And if you don't want to do the talking yourself, your brother Aaron will do it for you. I've already told him to come and meet you, and he's on his way. Whatever more could you possibly want?"

Moses was exceedingly reluctant, but at last he agreed.

"Oh all right," he said grudgingly. "I suppose I'll have to go."

So the bush became normal again, Moses put his shoes back on and went home to pack.

He said to Jethro, "Would it be all right if I went back to Egypt for a while to see how my family is?"

"Oh, by all means," said Jethro. "Have a nice time. Go in peace."

So, in fear and trepidation, Moses set off on the long walk back to Egypt.

Moses and Pharoah

t the time that Moses set out for Egypt, Aaron was on his way to Midian, and they met in the wilderness and continued together to Egypt, making a few plans.

"God says we've got to ask Pharaoh to give the Children of Israel a three-day weekend to go into the desert to pray," said Moses.

"Gracious," said Aaron. "He'll never agree to that, will he? What shall we do next?"

"Well," said Moses, "as far as I can gather, God has planned some plagues to make Pharaoh change his mind."

"Oh I see," said Aaron. "Well that should be interesting."

When they got to Egypt, they went to the Children of Israel and told them that God was going to rescue them. The Children of Israel believed them for some reason and were thoroughly delighted, naturally. So Moses and Aaron went to see Pharaoh.

Needless to say, Pharaoh had a totally different outlook on the entire scheme.

"Good morning, Pharaoh," said Moses. "God wants you to give the Israelites a three-day weekend to feast and pray."

"*What* did you say?" said Pharaoh. "A three-day weekend for *slaves?* You must be crazy. Whoever would do all the work? What an absolutely idiotic idea."

"Well," said Aaron," if you don't agree, God says there'll be some plagues."

"God? God?" said Pharaoh. "Who's He, I should like to know? I'm the god around here."

"God is the God of Abraham, Isaac and Jacob," said Moses. "And He says let His people go."

"What twaddle," said Pharaoh. "I've never heard of Him. Of course the Israelites can't have a holiday. In fact, they'd better work harder than ever making bricks. They shan't be given the straw they need to make the bricks with anymore. They'll have to find their own straw and still make just as many bricks. A three-day weekend, indeed."

So the poor Israelites had to work harder than ever and went to Moses and said, "Now look what you've done. Not only don't we get a long weekend, but we have to work even harder than before. You haven't helped one little bit."

So Moses went to God and said, "Didn't I tell you I'd bungle it? Look what's happened now. What do we do next?"

And God said, "Go to Pharaoh and throw down your crook so that it turns into a snake."

So back went Moses and Aaron to Pharoah, and they did as God had said. But Pharaoh called in his magicians, who were able to do exactly the same trick with their rods. And although Moses's rod-snake swallowed up all the Egyptian rod-snakes, Pharaoh was not the least bit impressed.

"Well, all right," said Moses. "If you want to be stubborn, that's your affair. But I warn you, all the water in Egypt will be blood tomorrow."

The Plagues of Egypt

T he next morning, according to instructions from God, Aaron went 'round all the Egyptians' rivers, lakes, pools, ponds and streams, smiting them with the rod, and all the water turned instantly to blood. And all the fish died, and the Egyptians had no water to drink or wash in, and they had to dig new wells.

Moses and Aaron visited Pharaoh again.

"What about that three-day weekend?" they said.

But the Egyptian magicians could do the same trick, too, so Pharaoh was still unimpressed.

Then Moses said, "Well, the next plague is going to be frogs. God says there will frogs everywhere — frogs in the soup, frogs in your wine, frogs where you want to sit, frogs where you walk, frogs under your pillow, frogs in your bed — frogs, frogs, frogs."

"So who cares," said Pharaoh. "Dear little things, frogs."

When the next day came, however, Pharaoh found that he really did rather care after all, and he sent for Moses and Aaron.

"All right, all right," said Pharaoh. "Enough is enough. Get your God to get rid of the frogs tomorrow, and you can all have your long weekend."

"Oh, thank you very much," said Moses and Aaron. "We will speak to God about it at once."

But as soon as the frogs had gone, Pharaoh began to think of all the work the Israelites did, and he changed his mind. He sent for Moses and Aaron again.

"I've changed my mind," he said to them. "You can't go after all."

"Oh honestly," said Moses and Aaron. "How annoying can you get? Well, God says the next plague will be nasty little lice crawling all over you and all your animals, and you'll all itch horribly."

The Egyptian magicians tried to make lice, too, but they couldn't, and they said to Pharaoh:

"This is the finger of God."

"I don't care," said Pharaoh, and he got angrier and angrier.

So God told Moses to go to Pharaoh again.

"God says let my people go, or tomorrow there'll be swarms of flies everywhere."

"Oh, do go away," said Pharaoh. "You bore me."

So the next day there were millions and millions of flies everywhere, all over Egypt and all over the Egyptians, but none of the plagues troubled the land of Goshen, where the Israelites lived. This must have annoyed Pharaoh considerably.

After a day of flies in his ears and eyes and nose and hair and food, Pharaoh sent for Moses and Aaron and once again said, "All right, you can have your long weekend. Just don't go too far away, so that you can get back quickly, and tell your God to take away these maddening flies."

"Thank you," said Moses and Aaron. "We certainly hope you don't change your mind this time."

But it will scarcely surprise you any more to learn that the moment the flies vanished, Pharaoh once again canceled the vacation.

So then God said to Moses, "Go and tell Pharaoh to let my people go, because if he doesn't then the next plague will be a murrain on all their cows, horses, donkeys, camels, oxen and sheep. In fact, it will be such a grievous murrain that the animals will probably die."

A murrain is a highly infectious disease, which animals in the olden days used to die from like flies, and Pharaoh should have been more considerate of his people than to let their animals die. But instead, he just grew more and more obstinate and hard-hearted, and all the more determined to keep the Israelites as slaves.

So God went on sending more plagues. After the murrain, all the Egyptians were covered with boils and blains, which were ugly great lumps all over their bodies. These not only looked extremely unattractive but must have hurt most hideously when the Egyptians sat down or stood up or lay down.

Next came a storm of hailstones so enormous that many of the Egyptians' crops were wrecked, and anyone foolish enough to go outside was promptly wrecked too. By now many of the Egyptians were pretty sick of the plagues and begged Pharaoh to let the Israelites go before all Egypt was ruined. But Pharaoh wouldn't do it.

After the hailstones came swarms and swarms of locusts, which are little creatures like grasshoppers that eat up every green leaf or blade of grass in sight. So millions of locusts came and ate all the leaves off the trees and any green crops the hail had missed. But still Pharaoh refused to let the Children of Israel have a long weekend, even though Egypt was a chaotic wreck.

The ninth plague was three days of total darkness throughout all Egypt. All day and all night long, for three days, the land lay in utter blackness. They could not see one another or even find the way out of their houses.

Then Pharaoh sent for Moses, and said, "Well, all right. Your God has won. You can go off for your three-day weekend and tell your God to stop plaguing us. But leave your cattle behind for us, because we are a bit short after that murrain."

"Oh no, that won't do, I'm afraid," said Moses. "We must take all our cattle and everything with us. God says so."

This made Pharaoh lose his temper completely.

"In that case you can't go," he said furiously, "and I never ever want to see your face again as long as I live. If you come bothering me one single other time, I'll have your head chopped off. Now begone this minute."

"I will not see you again," said Moses, "but you'll be sorry." And he went out, back to the Children of Israel.

The Tenth and Last Plague

od had told Moses that the tenth plague would be the last, because it would be so terrible that Pharaoh would tell His people to go at once.

So Moses went to the Children of Israel to give them instructions.

He said, "God says we'll be leaving in rather a hurry when the next plague comes, because it's going to have to be a really frightful one before Pharaoh will give up. So get packed and get picnics ready so that we can leave the minute Pharaoh says so. There won't be time to make proper bread with yeast in it, so just make quick, flat old bread that doesn't need time to rise. Have a final decent meal of roast lamb for supper, and be sure to make a mark on the outside of your doorposts."

So the Children of Israel packed and made picnics and marked their doorposts. And that night God sent the angel of death all through the land into every house except the houses with marked doorposts, which the angel passed over. But into the Egyptians' houses, the angel went, and the eldest sons of all the Egyptians died that night, and so did the eldest babies of all their pigs, sheep, goats, donkeys and camels. Even the firstborn sons of prisoners in dungeons died.

And Pharaoh's son died too.

At last, in the middle of the night, Pharaoh gave in and sent for Moses.

"Go," he said. "Go, all of you. Go at once and for heaven's sake don't ever come back."

So the Children of Israel took their luggage and their flat, unleavened bread, and left in the middle of the night. And God told Moses that the Israelites must remember that night forever.

"This is the night I brought you out of Egypt," said God. "Every year you must have a feast of roast lamb and flat bread, and call it Passover, because the angel of death passed over your houses."

And Moses said:

"Certainly. I will see that it is done. What a very good idea."

It has been done ever since.

Crossing the Red Sea

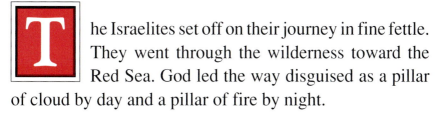he Israelites set off on their journey in fine fettle. They went through the wilderness toward the Red Sea. God led the way disguised as a pillar of cloud by day and a pillar of fire by night.

All went well for a while, but before very long they reached the Red Sea, and the Israelites immediately complained to Moses.

"Now look what you've done," they said. "We've walked for days and days and now here's the Red Sea. We can't walk across that. What are we supposed to do now? Fly? We might just as well have died in Egypt as walk all this way and then drown."

Moses said:

"Yes, I see what you mean. It does look a bit tricky. I'll talk to God about it."

So Moses talked to God about it, and God said that the whole thing was child's play. He sent a huge wind, which piled up the Red Sea into two heaps with a dry path in the middle. The Israelites calmed down and started to walk across.

But meanwhile, back in Egypt, Pharaoh had changed his mind yet once again.

"Why ever did I let them go?" he said. "Who's going to do all the work now?"

So he ordered up all his chariots and soldiers and sent them galloping at top speed after the Israelites. The Israelites heard the thunder of the oncoming Egyptians and saw the clouds of dust being kicked up by galloping hooves and wasted no time complaining to Moses again.

"What's the good of all this? Really, it's too inefficient. Look at all the trouble we went through to escape, and now we'll be caught again. Thoroughly pointless the whole thing seems."

Moses said he'd mention it to God, and God said He did wish by now they'd trust Him and will they please keep going? So they kept going and got across the Red Sea. The Egyptian army was halfway across, and, when the Israelites turned round to look, God told Moses to stretch his hand out over the sea. So he did. And the wind dropped. The wall of water on the left side crashed down. The wall of water on the right side crashed down. All the Egyptians were drowned. The Israelites sang.

Trials and Tribulations

At long last Pharaoh had to give up, and the Children of Israel were really free. They began their long search for the land of milk and honey that God had promised them. They walked for three days without finding any water, and when at last they came to some water, it was too bitter to drink. So, of course, instead of being grateful for small mercies and drinking it anyway, they went at once and grumbled to Moses.

"This water is perfectly revolting," they said. "Why ever did we leave Egypt? At least we had water there. What are you going to do about it, Moses?"

Moses said he would mention it to God.

"What about this revolting water, God?" Moses said. "The people say they can't drink it."

God explained that if they would put some branches of a nearby tree into the water, it would turn sweet. So they did, and it did. And they walked on.

After two or three months they were in a real wilderness and could find absolutely nothing to eat. They immediately wished they were back in Egypt and began to be most ungrateful to Moses about everything.

"We wish to God we were back in Egypt," they said to Moses. "Why did you drag us out of Egypt for this? We were expecting milk and honey, and here we are, starving. Our children are starving, our wives are starving, our animals are starving. *Do* something, can't you?"

"Oh dear, I'm so sorry," said Moses. "I'll see what plans God has for us."

"Look God," he said. "The people really are starving. They wish they were back in Egypt. Do you have any new ideas?"

"Yes," said God. "I'll rain bread crumbs down from heaven early every morning and send quails in every evening."

Quails are delicious, very tender little birds.

"Thank you," said Moses.

So Moses called the Children of Israel together and said, "God is going to rain down bread crumbs every morning and send quails in every evening, except on the seventh day. The seventh day is the one when God rests, so you must collect twice as much on the sixth day. But you must never collect more than you need, because that's greedy; and if you have any left over at the end of the day, it will grow worms and stink."

So down came the bread crumbs, and they were called manna and tasted rather like bread and honey. And in the evenings, in came the quails in plenty of time for supper. Needless to say, there were some people who were greedy and took too much, and sure enough it grew worms and stank dreadfully; so they probably did not do that again. Then there were others who were lazy and did not collect a double quantity on the sixth day and had to go hungry on the seventh day, because when they went out to gather their breakfast manna, there wasn't any. Let us hope they soon learned to follow God's simple instructions, because they were in the wilderness living on manna and quails for forty years it seems. (We must remember, however, that "forty" was their number meaning "a great many," in the same way we would say, "There are millions of children in my school" or "I've got millions of toys.")

Once again, the Children of Israel were without water in their journeying, and once again they became enraged with Moses and wished they were back in Egypt.

"I suppose you want us all to die, do you?" they raged.

So Moses said to God, "Quick, help me. The people are fearfully cross and ready to throw stones at me."

And God said, "Yes, of course. Take your rod, the same old rod that used to turn into a snake, and smite the rock in front of you and water will come out."

So Moses hit the rock and plenty of water came pouring out, and that problem was settled.

The next crisis was a battle. The Children of Israel came to Amalek, and the Amalekites started to fight them.

Then Moses spoke to a sensible man called Joshua and said, "Gather together some men who would be good at fighting, and fight the Amalekites tomorrow."

"Yes, all right," said Joshua, and he collected a small army.

The next morning Moses went up a little hill with Aaron and someone called Hur to watch the battle.

And it came to pass that whenever Moses held his arms up, the Israelites were winning. But if his arms ached and he put them down, then the Amalekites were winning. In the end they hit upon the sensible plan of Moses sitting on a rock while Aaron held up one arm and Hur held up the other. So the Children of Israel won their first battle against the Amalekites, and then Moses could put his arms down.

Aaron and the Golden Calf

O n went the Children of Israel, still searching for the land of milk and honey. They reached a wilderness called Sinai, which had a mountain in it also called Sinai. God told Moses to climb up the mountain for a private talk. He said He had a whole set of rules for the Children of Israel to go by, and He wanted to discuss them quietly with Moses first.

So Moses called Aaron to him and gave him some instructions.

"Oh hello, Aaron," said Moses. "God wants me to climb this mountain for a private talk and to give me some rules for the Israelites. So will you please look after every-thing for me while I'm gone?"

"Oh heavens yes, of course," said Aaron. "About how long will you be away do you suppose?"

"Forty days and forty nights, most likely," said Moses. "It's the usual length of time with us, isn't it. So goodbye now."

"Goodbye, have a nice time," said Aaron.

So off went Moses, mountain climbing, and Aaron began looking after things. Unfortunately, he was not as well qualified for the job as Moses supposed, and when the Children of Israel brought their complaints to him, he gave them the absolutely wrong answers. One day they came in with particularly grumpy complaints.

"Good morning, Aaron," they said. "We've been hanging around this old mountain for weeks and weeks, waiting for Moses to come back down, and we know not what has become of him. We don't think he'll ever come back. What do you think?"

"Oh dear," answered Aaron. "I really don't know what to think, I'm sure. He *said* he'd be back, but of course you can't ever tell."

"Our thoughts exactly," they replied, "and we don't even feel sure that God knows what He's up to either. What do you think?"

"Oh dear! Oh dear," said Aaron, getting more and more irresolute. "God seems to have done all right so far, don't you think? But I must say He is taking a bit of time now."

"Precisely," went on the Israelites. "We think God may not come back either, so here's our idea. We want you to make us a golden statue to pray to, like the ones they had in Egypt. It's much more fun praying to something you can see, don't you agree?"

"Oh dear, what a worry," said Aaron. "I really don't think I should do that."

"Well if you don't," they said, "we warn you there will be serious unrest. The people are tired of waiting."

"Oh dear, then I suppose I'll have to," said Aaron weakly. "Collect everyone's golden earrings and bracelets and necklaces and rings, and bring them to me."

So Aaron melted all their golden jewelry and made a golden statue of a calf. Perhaps there wasn't enough gold for a cow, or perhaps he thought it was more helpful to pray to a calf!

"Here you are, O Israel," he said to the Israelites. "Here's your god that brought you up out of Egypt. Tomorrow we'll have a feast to honor our god."

The Children of Israel were thrilled with the statue and got up early next morning to have a feast day. They danced joyfully round their mindless golden calf, and ate picnics and generally had a festive time.

But up on the top of the mountain, God saw what was happening and stopped what He was saying to Moses.

"Quick, quick," He said. "Hurry down, because the people are all behaving frightfully badly. In spite of everything I've done for them, they're all worshiping a foolish golden calf. I'm very, very cross indeed. How could they be so utterly idiotic? I think I'll just kill the lot of them and not bother with them anymore."

"Oh please don't do that," said Moses. "I mean, think what the Egyptians would say for a start. They'd say, 'What a silly idea rescuing all those Israelites from us just to burn them up in a fit of temper. How childish their God is.' And besides," went on Moses, "remember how you promised Abraham, Isaac and Jacob all those centuries ago that they'd have as many descendants as there are stars and that you'd give them a country of their own?"

"Oh yes, that's right, so I did," said God. "Well, all right, I'll forgive them, but all the same I'm pretty angry."

"Well I'll think up a punishment for them when I get down off the mountain," said Moses.

So Moses hurried down the mountain carrying two tablets of stone on which God had written the rules for the Children of Israel. But when he got close enough to see what was going on, he became very angry, too, and flung the stone tablets down in his rage and broke them. He spoke furiously to Aaron.

"Honestly, Aaron," he said, "what a perfectly disgraceful scene. How on earth could you be so feeble? God is simply furious, and look what you've made me do, too — break the rules."

"Oh dear, yes, I know," said Aaron. "It is rather awful, isn't it. But it's not my fault. The Children of Israel made me do it. They said they didn't think you were coming back. I couldn't help it."

"That's an absolutely rotten excuse," said Moses. "You're grown up, aren't you? Of course you could help it. 'Can't help it' is for babies. You're supposed to know better.

So go and grind up that useless statue into powder and make them all drink it in water to teach them a lesson."

So Aaron went and ground the statue into powder and gave the Children of Israel their costly medicine to drink. It must have tasted thoroughly revolting, and let us hope that Aaron had to take some, too.

Moses, of course, had to climb back up the mountain to get another set of rules from God to bring down.

These rules cover nearly a hundred pages of very small writing, which we don't need to go into here. Ten of these rules, however, are exceptionally well known and are called the Ten Commandments, and people all over the world have been struggling to go by them ever since, with a simply staggering lack of success.

The first of these commandments says, "I am the Lord thy God which brought thee out of Egypt out of the house of bondage. Thou shalt have none other gods but me."

("Thee" and "thy" and "thou" are old-fashioned words for "you," "your" and "you." Nearly four hundred years ago, when the Bible was first translated into English from Hebrew, Greek and Latin, these old-fashioned words were used by people in everyday life.)

The second commandment says that no one is to pray to statues — they must pray only to God!

Another instructs them to work for six days and rest on the seventh day and make it holy, because that's what God did when He made the world, according to the Israelites' legend of Creation. Before this commandment, there had been no specially kept holy day each week.

Then there are rules that say they must not kill, or steal, or tell lies about their neighbors, or covet anything at all that belongs to someone else. "Covet" means "badly want to have."

At first glance, all the rules sound very simple to keep. But this is deceptive, as you will see if you think carefully about each one separately.

Soon after, Aaron died, and God told Moses that if he wanted to see the land He'd promised them all, he'd better climb up a mountain called Abarim and look at it in the distance, because Moses, too, was going to die before they got there.

So Moses said, "Yes, all right. I'd like to have a look at it before I die. And who is going to take over from me?"

God said, "Joshua, the son of Nun, will take over from you."

So Moses handed over everything to Joshua, went up Mount Abarim, saw the Promised Land, and then died and was buried. It says he was a hundred and twenty when he died, but we know they weren't very good at counting. Or perhaps the years were shorter then than they are now. In any event, the Children of Israel wept for Moses for thirty days.

"And there arose not a prophet since in Israel like unto Moses, whom the Lord knew face to face."

PART TWO

Joshua and the Spies

he Promised Land that God had shown Moses was the land of Canaan, and now, with Joshua guiding them, the Children of Israel came close to Canaan. But the big snag about the place was that it was already full of other tribes and kings and cities that weren't at all anxious to belong to the Israelites. So it became necessary for the Israelites to fight many, many battles. When they remembered to obey God's rules, they won their battles. When they didn't, they didn't. To remind them of God's rules, Moses, before he died, had made them build the Ark of the Covenant of God. A covenant is a promise, and of course the promise God had made was His promise to Abraham, Isaac and Jacob.

The Ark of the Covenant had nothing to do with the ark Noah built. It was more like a portable temple, and everywhere the Israelites went, the Ark was carried with them by the priests. The priests were all Levites — that is, men of the tribe of Levi. Levi was one of Jacob's twelve sons, you remember, and God had picked this tribe to be the priests. After the golden calf fiasco, Moses realized that it would help a lot if the people had a visible reminder of God and His promise, so God had given Moses very particular instructions about building the reminder, and the Ark was the result. The commandments and other rules were all kept inside the Ark.

Now, after the death of Moses, God spoke to Joshua to cheer him up.

"Don't worry," He said. "I will be with you as I was with Moses. All this country before you is for my people. Only be strong and of good courage, because it's going to be pretty tough. Just stick to the rules, say your prayers, and you'll have success. Don't be afraid. I'll be with you."

"Well thank you very much," said Joshua. "That's a big comfort. I was really feeling pretty worried."

"I expect you'll manage," said God.

So Joshua sent for two men to go and do some spying in the city of Jericho, which was just across the river Jordan on whose banks they were all camping.

"Ah! Good morning, spies," said Joshua. "I need you to do some spying in Jericho for me, please. Go and stay in Rahab's house. She'll let you in all right. Strange men often stay in her house, so no one will notice you, and you can't miss her house — it's on the town wall."

In those days cities had strong walls built all around them to keep out enemies. They were so thick that houses were often built on them. There were gateways for coming in and going out, but these would be kept tightly shut and heavily guarded all night and also in times of danger.

"All right," said the spies. "We'll see what we can spy."

So off they went, and sure enough Rahab did let them in. But unfortunately, someone *did* notice them and went off at once to tell the king of Jericho.

"Sir! Sir!" said they to the king. "Two men of the Children of Israel are in the city spying. They're staying with Rahab. If you hurry, you can catch them."

So the king sent soldiers hurrying off to Rahab. But Rahab wasn't taking any chances. She hid the spies in her attic while she went to talk to the soldiers. She did not like soldiers much. They had probably been rude to her.

"Now then, my good woman," said the soldiers. "Where are those two strange men who came here? They're spies, and the king wants them. Come on, speak up."

So Rahab said, "Oh, yes, well, two men did come here, it's true, but I didn't know who they were or where they came from. In any case they've gone now. They went just as it got dark, so perhaps if you hurry, you can catch them. Heaven knows which way they went, but if you stop wasting time talking, you can probably catch up with them."

Luckily the soldiers were quite gullible and believed every word. They tore off into the night on their wild-goose chase. Rahab rushed up to the attic to tell the spies.

"They're looking for you," she said, "but I fooled them. Listen, everyone in Jericho is scared of you Israelites because we know your God is strong, and we've heard about the Red Sea and all that. So now I'll let you out of my window, down the city wall, by a rope, and you'd better hide in those mountains over there for two or three days until they've stopped looking for you. But since I've been so helpful and hidden you from the soldiers, could you please promise that when you capture this city, you won't hurt me or my father or my mother or my brethren or all my aunts and uncles and nieces and nephews?"

"Oh certainly," said the spies. "That's the least we can do for you — you've been more than helpful. But you will have to make sure your whole family is in this house at the time. We can't promise to save them if they're out of doors. And also, tie a bit of this red string to the window so that our men will know which house it is. Otherwise we can't guarantee anything. And of course, if you tell on us when we've gone, then we certainly won't bother to save you or your mother or your father or your brethren or any of the rest of them."

"Oh yes, of course," said Rahab. "I entirely understand."

So she let them out of her window, down the wall. They hid in the mountains for three days, until the soldiers had stopped searching for them, and then they went back to Joshua to report.

"It'll be fairly easy," they said. "All the people are scared stiff of us."

"Well it won't be all that easy," said Joshua. "After all it's got that great thick wall all around it. Still, I expect God'll think up some plan."

The Fall of Jericho

The Israelites were in no hurry to attack Jericho. They pitched camp and then peacefully celebrated their Passover feast. When the feast was over, the quails and manna stopped appearing each morning and evening. They were in the Promised Land now, God said, and could look after themselves.

Naturally, the people of Jericho were keeping their city gates firmly bolted and barred these days because they knew they were going to be attacked by the Israelites before long. Although they were scared of the Israelites, they felt fairly safe because their walls were so exceedingly thick and strong. But God had a most unusual plan for capturing Jericho, and he told it to Joshua. So Joshua told the people.

"Nobody is to say a word all day long," said Joshua. "The soldiers are going to march silently all around Jericho. The priests will carry the Ark, and seven priests will each carry a ram's horn trumpet. When they've gone all around Jericho, the seven priests will blow the seven trumpets. When you hear the trumpets, then you must all shout your loudest."

"Well, what a very funny way to capture a city," said the people.

"Yes," said Joshua, "it's quite a new idea."

So the next day they were all silent — though goodness knows how they stopped the babies and children from screaming and yelling. The soldiers and priests solemnly stalked around Jericho while everyone watched. Then when they blew the trumpets, everyone shouted and roared. What happened? Exactly nothing, except perhaps a few sore throats from shouting.

"Whatever was that all about?" they asked. "What's the idea here? What next?"

"Don't be in such a rush," said Joshua. "We're going around Jericho six days in a row blowing trumpets and shouting. It's God's scheme, so don't fuss."

So for six days, once a day, they marched around Jericho, blew ram's horn trumpets, and roared their loudest.

Before the seventh day, Joshua gave some final orders. Presumably God had said that they could overlook the rule about resting on the seventh day.

"Now today," said Joshua, "God says we are to march, blow, and shout seven times in a row. On the seventh time, you must shout fit to burst, because God says the city will be ours."

"Well, it still seems a funny way to capture a city," they said.

So seven times the army and the priests marched around Jericho. And seven times the trumpets were blown. And seven times the people shouted. But the seventh time they shouted themselves hoarse, and the walls of the city of Jericho collapsed with an enormous roar and crumbled to the ground, and the Children of Israel captured it. Rahab and her family were all saved, and Joshua became famous.

Deborah and Jael

fter the battle of Jericho, the Children of Israel won most of their battles because all the people they fought — the Ammonites, the Amorites, the Hittites, the Canaanites, the Hivites, the Jebusites, the Perizzites and lots of other "ites" — were so scared. So by the time Joshua died, he had allotted different parts of the country to the twelve tribes of Israel, who settled down and built and planted as a pleasant change from walking.

But after the death of Joshua, the Israelites became slightly lazy about keeping God's rules. So their neighbors began to defeat them in battle.

The Israelites had a succession of judges to tell them what God was thinking and to solve their disputes and problems. At the time of this story, their judge was a woman called Deborah. She lived under a palm tree by Mount Ephraim, and the Children of Israel came to her for judgment. But not enough of them had been coming because they were disobeying God, so the Canaanites kept defeating them. The captain of the Canaanite army was called Sisera, and he had nine hundred chariots of iron, which is a great many.

So the Israelites had a wretched time, and eventually they were sorry enough, and God forgave them and sent a message to Deborah to give to Barak, the Israelite captain. So Deborah sent for Barak.

"Good morning, Barak," said Deborah. "God says it's time for you to take the army to the river Kislion and defeat Sisera."

"Oh dear, yes, well, I'm sure you're right," said Barak, "but the whole thing makes me faintly nervous. I mean think of those nine hundred iron chariots for a start. I'm sure God's trustworthy and all that, but if you won't go with me, I won't go. If you'll go with me, then I'll go."

"Oh yes, certainly. Of course I'll go with you," said Deborah. "I'd be delighted. Though God tells me that as a matter of fact, it won't be you that'll finish off Sisera, it'll be some strange woman."

"Oh, really?" said Barak. "Fancy that! Will you let me know what day we should start?"

"Of course," said Deborah.

So the Canaanites and Israelites got their armies organized, and on the right day Deborah went to Barak and said:

"Up, Barak! This is the day, the Lord says. So get going."

Barak obediently went out with his army, and they completely defeated the Canaanites so that Sisera climbed down off his iron chariot and ran away on foot. While Barak chased off after the other chariots, Sisera ran to the tent of Jael, the wife of a friendly neighbor.

Jael saw Sisera coming and went out to meet him.

"Come in," she said. "You can trust me. I'll hide you."

So she covered him up with a mantle.

"Oh, thanks a lot," said Sisera. "I wonder if I could trouble you for some water? I'm really frightfully thirsty after all that fighting."

"By all means," said Jael, but gave him some milk instead and covered him up again.

A little while later Sisera said, "By the way, would you mind standing by the door of the tent, and if anyone asks for me, say you haven't seen me? I'm dreadfully tired, I find, and really don't want to be bothered with guests.

So Sisera went to sleep, and while he was fast asleep Jael took a tent peg and a hammer, and hammered the tent peg right into Sisera's temple. So that was rather the end of Sisera. He shouldn't have trusted her.

Shortly afterwards, Barak came along looking for Sisera.

"I know whom you're looking for," said Jael. "He's in my tent."

So Barak looked inside her tent, and sure enough there was Sisera, dead. Then Barak and Deborah sang a long song about it. There is a part that says: "He asked for water and she gave him milk; she brought him butter in a lordly dish." It sounds an attractive way to have butter.

So then the Children of Israel kept the rules, and all went well for a while. But for some reason they seemed to find it much harder to obey God once they had stopped walking and had settled down in the Promised Land. Perhaps it was from living so close to other tribes who did not have rules or bother about the Israelite's God, but instead had many, many strange gods and statues of their own.

Gideon

The next time the Children of Israel did evil in the sight of the Lord, it was the people of Midian who defeated them. For seven years the Midianites kept winning, and the Israelites grew very unhappy. They took to living in caves to hide; but then when they'd sown their seeds, the Midianites came and stole their harvest, so the Israelites were hungry as well as wretched.

Finally God decided to help. He sent an angel to sit under an oak tree. By the oak tree was a strapping young man named Gideon. Gideon was threshing some wheat by his winepress, where he had kept it hidden from the Midianites.

The angel said to Gideon, "The Lord is with thee, thou mighty man of valor."

"Oh, really? Are you sure?" asked Gideon. "I mean, if God's still bothering about us, why are we having such a beastly time with the Midianites? I know He brought us out of Egypt and all that, but it was years and years ago. He's surely got tired of us now and abandoned us to the Midianites."

Whereupon God said to Gideon, "No, no. I haven't abandoned the Children of Israel at all, and in fact, I've just picked you to go and save everyone from the Midianites."

"Good gracious," said Gideon in surprise. "Did you say you'd picked me? How can I possibly save Israel? I'm fearfully poor and couldn't possibly raise an army or anything."

But God said, "Oh, but I will be with you, so you'll easily manage."

"Well, I see," said Gideon, doubtfully. "In that case, would you mind giving me some sort of sign that it's really you and not my imagination?"

"By all means," said God. "Bring me some meat and cakes."

So Gideon brought out some meat and cakes.

"Right," said God. "Now put them on that rock."

Gideon put them on the rock, and then the angel touched them with his stick, and instantly fire came out of the rock and burned up the meat and cakes. Then the angel vanished, and Gideon realized that he really had been an angel, and he grew rather worried.

"Oh dear. Oh dear," said Gideon. "Now whatever will happen to me? I've seen an angel face to face. What does it all mean? Oh dear, what a worry."

But God said to him, "Oh, you needn't carry on so. You're not going to die. Now the first job I want you to do is to go and knock over the altar that's been built to the false god Baal in your father's woods." So Gideon said he would, but as he was rather scared, he waited until night and did it when no one was looking. And he built an altar to God instead. The Midianites were rather annoyed, but Gideon felt braver now and blew a very loud trumpet, and sent messengers to gather the soldiers of Israel.

When all the soldiers had arrived, Gideon didn't feel quite so brave again, and he said to God, "Look, I know you said I could save Israel with your help, but I don't quite believe it. If it's really true, could you do this small thing for me, please? I'm going to put this sheepskin out on the grass, and if, when I come to look at it in the morning, I find the grass bone dry but the sheepskin sopping wet with dew, then I'll believe you."

So Gideon left the fleece of wool out on the grass, and next morning when he looked, he found the grass perfectly dry but the fleece so full of dew that he wrung it out into a bowl. But he still did not feel quite happy and said to God, "I do hope you won't be cross with me, but do you think, just to make quite sure, that you could do the thing the other way around? That is, if I leave the fleece out again tonight, could you make the grass be all covered with dew, but the fleece be dry as bone?"

And God did just that. In the morning the grass was soaking wet, but the sheepskin was dry.

So then Gideon took all the hosts of people who had come to join him, and they pitched camp beside a well.

But God said to him, "You've got far too many people there. If you win a battle with that many people, everyone will say, 'Look how clever and brave we were to beat the Midianites,' and they'll quite forget about my having helped them. I'm afraid you will have to get rid of some of the men. Tell anyone who's scared that he may go home."

So Gideon did that, and twenty-two thousand of them were scared and went home. But that still left ten thousand, and God said, "You've still got far too many people left. We'll have to get rid of a lot more. I've got an idea. Take them all down to the water for a drink, and anyone who laps the water as a dog does, you can keep. Anyone who drinks any other way, send away."

So Gideon took them all down for a drink, and out of ten thousand men, only three hundred lapped the water like a dog. God said he could manage splendidly with only three hundred. So the rest went home.

The Battle against Midian

When night came, God said to Gideon, "Get up and go down to the enemy camp quietly because it will give you a good idea. If you're too nervous to go by yourself in the dark, take your servant Plurah with you."

Gideon was nervous, so he woke up his servant and together they crept off to the Midianites' camp to see what this good idea would be. He had every reason to be scared, really, because there were so many Midianites and Amalekites that they were like grasshoppers for multitude, and they had innumerable camels too.

When Gideon got to the camp, he heard two men talking together.

"I say," said one. "I had a most peculiar dream. I don't know what it means."

"What did you dream?" said the other. "Perhaps I can see the meaning for you."

You remember that they set a lot of store by dreams in those days, and anyone who could interpret them was highly popular, and probably frightfully busy.

"Well," said the first man. "This is my dream. I dreamed a cake of barley bread rolled into one of our tents and knocked the tent over so that it fell down."

Whereupon his friend said, "Oh, that obviously is the sword of Gideon, so your dream means that Gideon will win the battle and defeat us."

This extremely unlikely meaning for the dream seems to have been obvious to Gideon, too, because he said, "Thank you, God. That did indeed give me an idea."

And he rushed back to his army and woke them up.

"Come on. Get up," he said. "I've got an idea for beating the Midianites. Get a trumpet, each of you, and an empty pitcher and a lamp to put in the pitcher. Whatever I do, you do. When I shout, 'The sword of the Lord and of Gideon,' then you shout, 'The sword of the Lord and of Gideon,' too."

Then they stealthily crept to the outside of the Midianite camp. When they were all ready, they all at once blew their noisy trumpets, broke their pitchers, held their lamps up in their left hands, and shouted, all together, "The sword of the Lord and of Gideon!"

The Midianites were all asleep except for a few watchmen. So the appalling racket the Israelites were making woke them up with a dreadful jerk. They didn't know what on earth was going on, and in the confusion they all started killing each other and then running away from what seemed to them like innumerable maniacs blowing trumpets and yelling.

So the three hundred Israelites beat the hosts of Midian, and the Israelites were so pleased that they asked Gideon and his son and his son's son, too, to rule over them. But Gideon said, "Oh no. I won't rule over you at all. God will."

So they had peace for forty years.

Jephthah's Vow

Again the children of Israel ignored the rules, particularly the one about not having any other gods but God. In fact, they really went to town over this one. They prayed to a god called Baal, and a god called Ashtaroth; they prayed to the gods of Syria, the gods of Zidon, the gods of Moab, the Ammonite gods, and the gods of the Philistines. They must have been kept extremely busy with all those gods!

God was exceedingly angry with His people for being so weak-minded, and He allowed the Philistines and Ammonites to defeat them and to be mean to them for eighteen years.

Then, at long last, from the depths of their misery, the Israelites turned to God and said, "Oh dear, we really have sinned badly, twice over — once because we forgot you, and again because we served all those other gods."

But God was still angry.

"Look," He said, "didn't I save you from the Egyptians and the Amorites and the Zidonians and the Amalekites and the Midianites? Whenever you've asked me, haven't I saved you? And look at the thanks I get. You forget me. So I won't help you anymore. You've chosen all those other silly gods, so go and cry to them. Let them help you. I'm fed up."

This really alarmed the Israelites, and they said, "Oh, please, God, don't leave us. We'll give up the useless gods at once, and we'll bear whatever punishment we deserve, but please help us now, please, please."

"Oh very well," said God. "I'll help you. Go and get Jephthah to lead you."

This was rather embarrassing for the Israelites, because they had all been mean to Jephthah when he was a boy and had teased him and said his mother wasn't married. It was true, she wasn't married. But it could hardly have been Jephthah's fault. Nevertheless, they would have nothing to do with him and even turned him out of his house. In spite of all that, or perhaps because of it, Jephthah had grown up very strong and brave.

Anyway, the leaders had no choice but to do what God said. They went to Jephthah and said, "Will you please come and be our leader against the Ammonites?"

"Well, why should I?" said Jephthah. "You were nasty to me before and turned me out of my father's house and hated me. Now you expect me to organize your war! Frankly, no, I don't think I will."

"Oh please do," they said. "You will be a marvelous general, and you can be the head leader over all of us."

"Well," said Jephthah, "suppose we win, what then? Will I go on being top man, or will you go back to being mean again?"

"Oh, you can go on being top," they said. "We promise you can."

"Then I'll fight the battle," said Jephthah. "But mind you keep your promise."

So off went Jephthah to see to the war, and he did very well indeed and won battle after battle. Before his last and biggest battle, he made a vow to God. A vow is an extra solemn promise, and a vow to God, of course, would be the most solemn promise of all.

"If you let me win this last big battle, God," said Jephthah, "then I vow I'll burn up the first thing I see when I get back to my house, as a sacrifice to you."

What Jephthah had in mind was probably something in the nature of a chicken or a goat, but unfortunately things worked out rather differently.

They won their battle, defeating their enemies thoroughly, and Jephthah returned home in a very happy frame of mind. But what was the first thing that he saw when he got there? A chicken or a goat? Oh no. The door opened, and down the path, dancing and singing and gay as a lark, came Jephthah's one and only child, a daughter whom he adored.

"Hello, father," she said. "How lovely to have you home again. I am so happy to see you. I've missed you so much."

"Oh, alas!" cried Jephthah, and instantly he ripped his clothes. They always ripped their clothes in those days when they were sad. His daughter was amazed and alarmed.

"Whatever's the matter, father?" she asked. "Aren't you glad to see me? Why are you ripping your clothes?"

Jephthah said, "I'm ripping my clothes because I promised God I'd burn up for him the first thing I saw when I got back, and unfortunately the first thing I saw was you. But a vow is a vow, so I'll have to burn you."

Naturally, his daughter was rather upset, but she didn't argue. She understood how solemn a vow was.

"Oh dear," she said. "Could I have two months to visit all my friends and say goodbye, do you think?"

"Oh yes. You certainly can do that first," said her father.

So she spent two months visiting her friends and saying goodbye, but after that I fear Jephthah had to keep his vow. He was probably a lot more careful before he made any other vows. He was the judge of Israel for six years after that and then he died. So at least the Israelites kept their promise to him, too.

Samson and Delilah

Time passed. Judges came and went. Battles were won and lost. At this point the Philistines were the chief enemy of the Israelites. There was a very strong Israelite called Samson, whom the Philistines badly wanted to capture but couldn't because he was so strong. Once he had killed a thousand Philistines with just the jawbone of a donkey, so you can see why he wasn't tremendously popular with them. But they were scared of him because of his unusual strength. At last they decided to ask his girlfriend, Delilah, to help.

"Look, Delilah," they said, "get Samson to tell you what it is that makes him so strong, so that we can work out a way to capture him. If you do, we'll give you eleven hundred pieces of silver.

Of course Delilah should immediately have said, "Certainly not. I wouldn't dream of telling you how you can capture my boyfriend."

But she didn't. She said, "Yes. All right. I'll try. But it's supposed to be a secret, you know, so he might not tell me."

"Oh, he'll surely tell you," they replied. "After all, you are his girlfriend."

So Delilah, who seems to have been a very sneaky, underhanded sort of a girl, went to Samson and said, "Do tell me, what is the secret of your strength? What would anyone have to do to make you as weak as an ordinary man?"

But Samson didn't tell, because it was a secret. Instead, he said, "Oh, just tie me up with seven fresh willow branches and then I'll be as weak as a kitten."

So Delilah tied him up with seven fresh green willow branches. When he was well bound up, she suddenly shouted at him, "Look out, Samson! The Philistines are upon you!"

Whereupon Samson leapt to his feet, broke his bonds and rushed out to find the Philistines. So she knew he hadn't told her the truth.

"Why did you lie to me?" she asked. "You made a fool of me. Do tell me the truth, please. After all, I am your girlfriend. Don't you love me? Don't you trust me?

So Samson said, "Well, if I were tied up with new ropes, I'd be weak."

Then Delilah tied him with new ropes, but when she again shouted, "Help! Samson! The Philistines are here!" Samson snapped the ropes as if they had been threads or cobwebs.

Delilah was furious at being tricked again, but she pretended she wasn't.

"Oh Samson, you fooled me again," she said. "Aren't you clever. But please, *please* tell me the really true secret of your strength."

To keep her quiet, Samson said, "Well, if you tie my hair to the beam in the ceiling, then I'll be weak."

So Delilah tied his hair to the beam, but he just walked away with the beam and all still attached to his hair, and Delilah knew he'd fooled her again.

"How can you say you love me when you won't tell me this one simple little secret?" said Delilah. "Don't you love me really? Three times you've lied to me and haven't told me. It's not nice."

Well, she wasn't really being very nice, either, was she?

Anyway, day after day, night after night, she went on at him like that. "You don't love me," and, "Why do you have secrets from me?" Day in, day out, she went on at him, until Samson simply couldn't stand it anymore. And instead of telling her to be quiet and go away, he stupidly told her the real secret of his great strength.

"My hair has never been cut in all my life," he said. "If my hair were shaved, I'd be weak. Now stop bothering me."

And so, when he was asleep, Delilah shaved his hair off, and the Philistines captured him easily because he was no longer strong. They paid Delilah eleven hundred pieces

of silver and took Samson off to prison, and he couldn't help himself. They put his eyes out so that he was blind, and then they chained him up and made him grind corn, and left him there.

One day, a long while later, when they were having a big feast, the Philistines said, "Why don't we get that silly, weak, blind Samson up out of his dungeon to amuse us at our party? He is so weak and feeble he might make us laugh, don't you think?"

So Samson was led up into the banquet hall, which was an enormous room with pillars to keep up the roof. In fact, it must have been a huge house altogether, because there were three thousand Philistines in it at the time, and they all thought it would be a good joke to laugh at Samson, who was too weak to do anything. Or so they thought. What they didn't realize was that as his hair had grown again, so had his strength. Because he couldn't see, Samson asked them to put each of his arms around a pillar to hold himself up. And they did, and they laughed to see him so weak that he couldn't stand by himself.

But Samson prayed to God and said, "Help me this last time, please God. I don't mind dying too if I can kill all these Philistines with me."

So Samson summoned all his strength and pulled the two pillars toward each other, and before the Philistines realized what was happening, the entire house collapsed on top of them as easily as a house of cards. And Samson and the three thousand Philistines all died.

Ruth

nce, during a famine, one of the Israelites de-cided to leave his home in Bethlehem and live in the land of Moab until the famine was over. He was called Elimelech, and he took with him his wife, Naomi, and his sons, Chilion and Mahlon. They got so used to living in Moab that they stayed there, and when the boys grew up, they married Moabite women, one called Orpah and one called Ruth.

Then, for some utterly unknown reason, Elimelach and Mahlon and Chilion all died, and the three women were left alone. They were quite upset, naturally, and decidedly lonely — especially Naomi, who began to think of the land she had left so long ago.

"Well, girls," she said one day to her daughters-in-law, "I think perhaps I shall go back to my own people in Bethlehem, seeing as how things have turned out so badly now."

"We'll come with you," said her daughters-in-law.

"Oh, good," said Naomi. "I'll certainly be glad of the company. It's a long, boring walk all by yourself."

So off they set; but then after a while Naomi realized that although she would be going back to old friends, Orpah and Ruth would both be going to a strange land full of strange people. So she said to them, "You know, I think it would probably be best for you if you both went back to your own homes, really, and I hope God will be as kind to you as you were to my sons."

Then Orpah and Ruth both started to cry.

"No, no," they said through their tears. "We'll stay with you."

"No, no," said Naomi. "You'd get lonely and bored. Go back. Find new husbands. Start a new life."

Then they all cried some more at the thought of parting, and Orpah decided that Naomi was right. She kissed her mother-in-law goodbye and went home. She was never heard of again.

But Ruth said, "It's no good trying to make me go, too. For whither thou goest, I will go; and where thou lodgest, I will lodge; thy people shall be my people and thy God my God. Where thou diest, will I die and there will I be buried."

This is a beautiful way of saying, "No, I won't go home. I will stay with you for the rest of your life."

So Naomi could see that it was no good trying to make Ruth go home, and they both went on together to Bethlehem. When they eventually arrived, people came out to greet them.

"Good gracious me!" they said in surprise. "Is this Naomi come back at last? How amazing! How are you, my dear? And how have you been? What brings you back after all these years? Who is this charming maiden with you? What has become of your husband and sons?" And other questions of the same ilk.

"Well, things didn't turn out so well at the end," said Naomi. "My husband and two sons all died, so I decided to come home. This is one of my daughters-in-law from Moab. She is Ruth, and she decided to stay with me and keep me company."

"Oh you poor things," said the neighbors. "How sad, but welcome home anyway."

Now it so happened that many of the fields around Bethlehem were owned by a very rich man called Boaz. It also happened that Boaz was a cousin of Naomi's dead husband. So Naomi said to Ruth, "Why don't you go gleaning in one of Boaz's fields and see if Boaz notices you?"

And Ruth said she would.

In the old days, before farm machinery, all the harvest was cut and carried by hand, and of course quite a lot got dropped. So the women were allowed to go and pick up as much as they could of what was dropped, entirely free. This was called gleaning, and naturally the more the women picked up, the more free flour they could grind for making bread.

So Ruth went gleaning, and Boaz noticed her at once.

"Who is that beautiful strange maiden out gleaning today?" he asked the foreman.

"Oh, that's Ruth, the Moabite woman," said the foreman. "She came with Naomi."

Then Boaz said to Ruth, "I'm so glad to see you. You can glean as much as you like in my fields, and I'll tell the workman to give you water when you're thirsty, and you can join the other women at the free lunch."

"Oh, how kind you are," said Ruth. "Thank you very, very much."

"Don't mention it," said Boaz. "You're very welcome."

"What's more," he added to himself, "you're very beautiful."

So he told the men who were harvesting to drop some wheat and barley on purpose for Ruth to glean.

Naomi was delighted when Ruth told her how kind Boaz had been.

"Good," she thought to herself. "Perhaps my little plan will work."

Naturally you can guess her little plan, can't you?

Next Naomi said to Ruth, "Why don't you go and rest in that barn over there for a while? I expect all that gleaning has made you tired."

So Ruth went and rested in the barn, and who should come along to rest, too, as Naomi had known he would, but Boaz himself! The little scheme was working well.

"Oh Ruth," said Boaz. "You're just the person I wanted to see. I find that you are quite a close relation to me through your husband who died, and one of our laws from Moses says that you ought to marry a close relation. I'd just love to marry you myself because you are such a beautiful damsel, but unfortunately I find there's another man closer still who has to have first chance. So I can't do anything about it until I've seen him. But if he's already fixed up or too busy, how would you like to marry me?"

"Oh, it would be simply lovely," said Ruth. "Thank you very much indeed."

So Ruth went home to tell Naomi, and Boaz went to the gate to waylay the other kinsman. It seems he didn't know the man's name, because when he appeared, Boaz called out, "Ho, such a one! Turn aside and sit down by me for a while." Which means, "Hey you! Come here a minute." But somehow "Ho, such a one" doesn't seem quite as rude as "Hey you!"

Anyway, the man sat down by Boaz, and they had a man-to-man discussion.

"Look here, old chap," said Boaz. "I thought you should know that Naomi wants to sell a piece of land that belonged to her husband, our cousin Elimelech, and if you want it, you get first choice. Do you want it?"

"Oh yes, I do want it," said the man.

"Well," said Boaz, "there's more to it than that, because on the day that you buy the land, you'll have to marry Ruth, Naomi's daughter-in-law. She goes with the land."

"Oh well, that's different," said the man. "I don't think I could marry her. It would make everything much too complicated. Why don't you buy the land and marry Ruth, instead of me?"

"Thank you very much," said Boaz. "I'd love to. Are you perfectly sure now?"

"Yes, indeed," said the man. "Here is my shoe."

And he gave Boaz his shoe. No, he had not gone crazy. It seems to have been their way of sealing a bargain instead of signing a contract. Presumably, if anyone later on had wanted to dispute Boaz's right to the land and Ruth, then Boaz could have shown them his cousin's shoe to prove that his cousin had agreed. They couldn't have made many bargains, though, or their houses would have been stuffed with odd shoes.

So Boaz went to the elders of Bethlehem and said, "I have bought Elimelech's field from Naomi, and I'm going to marry Ruth."

"Well, we hope you'll be happy and have loads of children, " they said.

So Boaz and Ruth got married, and Naomi's scheme had worked. We don't know if they had loads of children, but we do know that they had one son. He was called Obed, and his grandmother Naomi doted on him. When Obed grew up and married, he had a son called Jesse, and Jesse grew up to be the father of David. So Ruth was David's great-grandmother. If Ruth had gone back to Moab with Orpah, the whole of the rest of the history of the world would have been quite different because David's most famous descendant was Jesus.

Samuel and Eli

ow we come to the story of one of the most famous and the best of all the judges of Israel. He was also the last. His name was Samuel.

There was a man called Elkanah who had two wives, Hannah and Peninnah. Elkanah loved Hannah the best, but in spite of that, Hannah was sad because she didn't have any children and Peninnah had several. In those days there was no problem of population explosion, and women who didn't have children were apt to be despised by women who did. Sons were particularly popular. Peninnah was extremely mean to Hannah about it.

"What a useless woman you are, aren't you?" she would say. "You haven't got even one wretched child, and look how many I've got. Ha, ha, you hopeless, feeble woman."

One morning Hannah was so upset by this that she burst into tears and couldn't eat. Elkanah found her weeping and said, "Why are you weeping and not eating? What's the matter? Tell me everything."

So Hannah told him, "Peninnah is being mean to me because I haven't got any children and she's got lots, and I do wish I had a baby boy, oh dear, oh dear." And she went on crying.

Elkanah tried to comfort her because he loved her dearly and hated her to be so sad.

"Oh don't be unhappy," he said. "I love you a lot and I don't mind that you haven't got any children. Aren't I nicer to you than ten sons would be? Please cheer up."

But Hannah couldn't cheer up. So she went to the temple to pray. And she made a vow to God in her prayers.

"Please, God," she said, "let me have a baby boy. If you do, I promise I'll never cut his hair; and when he's old enough, I'll give him back to you to work for you in the temple, because I am really going frantic without any children."

You see, in those days if men didn't cut their hair, it meant they were holy.

Now it so happened that Eli, the priest, saw Hannah praying so desperately, and he jumped to the conclusion that she was drunk. He spoke to her kindly but very sternly, saying, "How long are you going to go on like this, you poor woman? I think you should give up drink altogether, and certainly you shouldn't come to the temple in such a drunken state."

"Oh good gracious," said Hannah, "I'm not drunk at all. I'm simply wretched, that's all, so I was praying rather desperately about something."

"Oh, I see," said Eli. "Well I do beg your pardon, and I certainly hope that God will give you whatever you were asking for."

So Hannah went home and stopped crying and started eating and tried to take a more cheerful view of life. And, sure enough, God did give her what she had asked for. After a suitable length of time, she had a darling little baby boy, and she was overjoyed. She called him Samuel, and she sang a very long song to God because she was so happy.

When Samuel was about five or six years old, Hannah took three bullocks, some flour, a bottle of wine and Samuel, and went back to Eli. She said to Eli, "Oh, my lord, I'm Hannah, the woman you thought was drunk a few years ago. This is the boy I was praying for. God answered my prayer, so I have brought him here to work for you in the temple because I promised him to God. Here he is. He is called Samuel, and I'll bring him a new coat every year."

"Oh how perfectly delightful," said Eli. "I am getting quite old now and would be glad to have some help. I fear my own sons are precious little use."

In fact, his sons were very wicked indeed, as we shall see.

So Hannah went home and had five more children in due course, and there was no more nonsense from Peninnah.

Samuel worked in the temple helping Eli, and Eli grew old and his eyes waxed dim. Samuel was good at his work and always tried to do what God wanted.

One night, ere the lamp of God went out in the temple, an unusual thing happened. Samuel was lying down, almost asleep, when he heard a voice call, "Samuel!" Naturally he thought it was Eli, and he jumped up and ran to Eli, saying, "Yes, Eli, here I am. What can I do for you?"

Eli was amazed and said, "Whatever do you mean? I didn't call you. Go back to bed."

So Samuel went back to bed. But again he heard the voice say, "Samuel!" and again he went to Eli.

"Here I am, Eli," he said, "because you *did* call me."

"No," said Eli, "I didn't call you. You must be dreaming. Go to sleep again."

So yet a third time Samuel started to go to sleep, and yet a third time he heard his name being called, and yet a third time he went back to Eli. This time Samuel was thoroughly perplexed, but this time Eli was unperplexed because he had realized what was going on.

"You really, really did call me," said Samuel. "I really, really heard it most distinctly."

"Well, no," said Eli. "I really didn't call you. But I know what is happening now. It must be God calling you.

If He calls again, you must say, 'Speak, Lord, for thy servant heareth,' and then listen to His message."

"Oh yes, all right," said Samuel. "I'll do that."

Eli was perfectly right. It was God calling. Samuel went back to bed, and before long he heard the voice calling his name again, so he said, "Speak, Lord, for thy servant heareth."

"Good," said God. "I've got a message for you that will make your ears tingle."

The message was that Eli's sons were so ghastly that they were going to be killed in battle. Samuel was a trifle upset about the message, because he knew that Eli would ask him about it in the morning, and he felt a little awkward about the whole thing.

Sure enough, just as Samuel was opening up the temple next day, Eli came to him and said, "Good morning, Samuel, my child. Did God give you a message last night?"

Samuel was dreadfully embarrassed and tried to pass it all off rather lightly.

"Well, yes. Yes, He did, actually. Um . . . yes. Well, it was nothing much, really, you know. Just this and that."

Naturally Eli was not a bit deceived, and said, "Don't be afraid. I won't blame you. But tell me all."

So then Samuel told him the whole thing. "Well, I'm afraid God said that your sons have become so evil that thy will be killed in battle."

And Eli said, "Oh dear. I was afraid it might be that. Well, God must do what He thinks is right, and I know my sons are very vile and wicked."

And it was just as God had said. Several years later Eli's sons were killed fighting the Philistines. The worst part of it was that because they were the priest's sons, they were the ones with the Ark, so the Philistines stole the Ark. All the children of Israel were unhappy; but luckily the Ark brought the Philistines such fearfully bad luck that they eventually sent it back to the Israelites with a present of jewels to boot!

Eli was more upset by the loss of the Ark than by the death of his sons, and he died when they told him about it. Anyway, he was ninety-eight and had been judge of Israel for forty years. Samuel was grown up by now and was very good and holy, and God often talked to him. So he became the judge of Israel.

Samuel and Saul

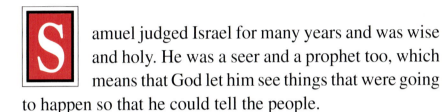amuel judged Israel for many years and was wise and holy. He was a seer and a prophet too, which means that God let him see things that were going to happen so that he could tell the people.

One day the Children of Israel came to Samuel and said, "You've been an excellent judge and never taken bribes or anything, but your sons are bad men, and we don't want them to be our judges after you. In fact, we would like you to pick someone to be our king. We think we'd like to have a king, like all the surrounding tribes."

And Samuel said, "Well, God says that's a rotten idea, but He'll choose you a king if you insist. Just don't blame Him when the kings grow greedy and vile and lead you into trouble."

"Oh no, we won't," they said. "We're sure we'd like a king."

Now there was a man of the tribe of Benjamin called Kish, who was very strong. He had a son called Saul, who was a lot taller than anyone else in Israel.

One day all Kish's donkeys seemed to be lost, and as he needed them, he said to his son, "Oh Saul, I wonder whether you would please take a servant with you and go and look for my wretched donkeys? I do rather need them."

"Oh but certainly," said Saul, and off he set. But though they searched high and low, not a trace of donkey did they find. So at the end of several days, Saul said to the servant, "We'd better go home I think, otherwise my father will stop worrying about the boring donkeys and start worrying about us."

"Yes," said the servant. "But actually I understand that Samuel, the man of God, is in this city. I believe he can see everything that's going to happen. Why don't we go to see him? He might be able to give us some sort of hint about where the donkeys are, don't you think?"

"Well, yes, what a good idea," said Saul. "The only snag about it is that I haven't got a present to give him, and I don't quite like to ask for free advice."

"Oh, that's all right," said the servant. "As it happens, I've got some silver handy. You can borrow it if you like."

"Oh, yes, indeed," said Saul. "Thank you very much. Let's go."

So they went up the hill to the city's well, where they found the usual charming maidens drawing water.

"Good day, charming maidens," said Saul. "Is the seer here, do you know?"

"Oh yes," said the charming maidens. "He's having a feast here today. If you hurry, you might be in time to get a bite to eat, too.

"Thanks a lot," said Saul, and off they hurried.

One of the first people they met was Samuel, but as they didn't know him, Saul said, "Excuse me, could you please tell me where the seer is?"

The very instant that Samuel saw Saul, God said in Samuel's ear, "Ah. This is the man I told you about last night. You can pick him to be the king."

So Samuel said, "Oh, I'm the seer actually. I've been expecting you. Won't you come and have lunch with me? And don't worry about those donkeys, they've been found. But God says you can be the first king of Israel."

Saul was slightly surprised, as well he might be, and said, "Oh, really? Are you sure? Why me, I wonder? After all, I belong to the tribe of Benjamin, which everyone knows is the least important tribe. How very unexpected."

"Well, if you don't believe me," said Samuel, "let me tell you what will happen on your way home. First you will meet three men, one carrying three kids, one carrying three loaves, and one carrying a bottle of wine. After that, when you get to the next city, you'll meet a collection of people singing and playing harps and prophesying, and what's more, you'll start prophesying too, and the spirit of God will come to you and you'll feel a new man. And when you get to Gilgal wait there for seven days, and I'll come and tell you what to do."

"Well, it really sounds all most unlikely," said Saul. "But since you're a famous seer, I expect you must be right."

And, of course, Samuel was right. Saul met all the people and did all the things that Samuel had said. Everyone was surprised to hear Saul prophesying, since prophesying means telling the future. And they said, "Good heavens, whatever has happened to Saul? Have you heard him? Is he a prophet now, too?"

Then Saul met his uncle, who said, "We've found the donkeys."

"Yes," said Saul, "I know. I met Samuel and he told me."

But he never mentioned the bit about being king. Perhaps he was still a little doubtful about it.

Then Samuel called all the Children of Israel together and said, "Thus saith the Lord God of Israel. He thinks you have rejected Him who saved you and that you want a king instead. Well, here's your king."

Then when they saw how handsome and tall Saul looked, they all said, "God save the king."

"Thank you very much," said Saul. "Now it's time to go home."

Samuel and David

So Saul became the first king of Israel, and the people were pleased. He won a lot of battles and was popular. But after a while he stopped keeping the commandments, and altogether got too big for his boots.

Therefore Samuel went to Saul one day and said, "Why aren't you obeying God any more?"

And Saul said, "What d'you mean? I'm making hundreds of burnt offerings to God, so what's He so annoyed about?"

Samuel said, "Do you mean you've grown so conceited that you've forgotten that obeying God is more important than burnt offerings? Any fool can make a burnt offering: you just burn it and say it's for God. But burnt offerings bore God a lot. He'd much rather people use their brains than burn things. And He says stubbornness is wicked. So since you aren't listening to God anymore, He won't have you for king much longer."

Then Samuel went away and never saw Saul again, because he was so disappointed in him. And God wished

He'd never chosen Saul to be king, so He set plans afoot for a replacement.

"Come along, Samuel," said God. "Stop wasting time worrying about Saul. We've got to find the next king. Go to Bethlehem now. There's a man there called Jesse who's got loads of sons. I think one of them will do for king."

"Well, but how can I do that?" asked Samuel. "If Saul hears about it, he'll kill me for sure."

"Well, you don't have to tell him, do you?" said God. "Go and have a feast with Jesse anyway, and I'll tell you what to do next."

So Samuel obediently set off. The people in Bethlehem were rather nervous to see him coming, in case they had done something to annoy God and Samuel was coming to tell them. The elders of the town went out to meet him.

"Good afternoon, Samuel," they said in trembling tones. "Are you here on business or pleasure?"

"Oh, purely pleasure," said Samuel. "I thought I'd like to have a feast with you."

"Oh good, yes, splendid, by all means," they said with smiles. "Please come and join us. We'd love to have you. We were just going to begin."

Then Samuel asked Jesse to introduce his sons to him.

"Well," said Jesse, "this is the eldest. He's called Eliab."

Samuel felt sure Eliab must be the one God wanted for king, because he was so handsome. But God said that he might look like a Greek god on the outside, but inside he looked simply terrible, and it's the inside that counts.

The next son was called Abinadab, and the one after him was Shammah. But God said to Samuel, "No, no. Not them."

Eventually seven sons had been introduced to Samuel, and God had said no to each one, so Samuel was a trifle puzzled.

"Well, that's a splendid family of strapping sons you have there," he said to Jesse. "Is that the lot? Or have you got any more anywhere?"

"Oh," said Jesse, "there is one more, but he's quite young, and he's looking after the sheep at the moment."

"Ah, I see," said Samuel. "Well, let's not have the feast without him."

So Jesse sent for his youngest son, who came in very out of breath from hurrying and rather red in the face too. But he was a good-looking lad, and God said to Samuel, "That's the one."

"Hello, my boy," said Samuel. "What's your name?"

"Oh, I'm David," said the boy.

Then Samuel explained that God had picked him to be the next king.

"Oh, I see," said David.

So then the Spirit of the Lord came upon David, but at about the same time it left Saul, who grew progressively more bad-tempered and unattractive.

At last Saul's servants could do nothing with him when he got upset, and they suggested it might help if someone came and played songs to him on the harp.

"Oh, all right," said Saul, "but make sure he plays in tune, for goodness sake."

"I know a boy who plays very well," said one servant. "That's David, the youngest son of Jesse."

"Fetch him, then," ordered Saul.

So whenever Saul got in a temper, they sent for David to play the harp. Goodness knows who looked after the sheep meanwhile. David played very well and Saul was soothed. The songs David sang are the ones we now call Psalms. There are a hundred and fifty of them. Some are songs of praise to God, some are songs of war, some are of comfort. The best known is probably the twenty-third, "The Lord is my Shepherd."

Saul grew fond of David, and Saul's son, Jonathan, was David's best friend.

David and Goliath

T he chief enemy of the Israelites at this time was the Philistines. They had decided to fight King Saul's army and had pitched their army on a mountain overlooking a valley. Saul's army was on the opposite side of the valley, also on a mountain. Some of David's elder brothers were soldiers in Saul's army.

The Philistines had on their side a gigantic man from Gath, called Goliath. He simply petrified all the Israelites by coming out of his tent and shouting at them.

"Hey, all you wet Israelites," he bawled. "I am the giant Goliath. Choose someone to fight me, you pusillanimous weaklings. Then if he wins, we'll all be your servants; but if I win, you'll all be our servants." Pusillanimous, by the way, means cowardly.

When Saul and the Israelites heard this, they were terrified and went into their tents and hid. Goliath roared with mirth.

This disgraceful scene was repeated for forty days, and no one was brave enough to try to fight the giant. David, meanwhile, was at home looking after the flocks. On the forty-first day Jesse sent for him and said, "Hello, David, will you please take these ten loaves and this corn to your brethren in the army, and give these ten cheeses to their captain. Army food is probably pretty terrible, so they'll be grateful. Then come back and tell me how your brothers are and what's going on."

So David left the sheep with a keeper and hurried off happily, hoping to see a jolly battle. He was just giving the provisions to his brothers when Goliath came out again to bellow at them.

"Ho! Ho! you feeble, useless wretches!" he shouted. "Haven't you found anyone brave enough to fight me yet? Goodness, what a hopeless, pathetic lot of drips you are."

David was simply amazed to see all the Israelites quivering with fright and slinking back into their tents.

"What's going on here?" he demanded. "Why doesn't someone fight this boastful, great hulking oaf instead of letting him bawl at you like that? What's the matter with everyone?"

Because his brother Eliab was feeling so scared, he was cross with David and said furiously, "What are *you* doing here, you tiresome brat? I know how naughty you are. You've come just to watch the battle, haven't you. Well, you can just go away."

"What have I done now?" asked David, rather reasonably. "I only said, why doesn't someone fight this complacent great half-wit Philistine."

"Well, if you must know," said another brother, "it's because we're all much too scared, that's why. Can't you see how huge he is, you silly? He'd kill us in a twinkling."

"But that's simply absurd," said David. "I'll go and fight him myself. Someone at least ought to try."

"*You?*" said a brother. "Don't be so utterly idiotic. You're much too young, and besides you haven't got any armor."

"Armor?" said David. "Who on earth needs armor? I killed a bear and a lion that were after our sheep once, and I never had any armor. God will help me."

"Well, you conceited, stuck-up ninny," said a brother. "Who do you think you are, pray? You are just a silly little show-off shepherd boy, that's who."

But by now someone had told Saul that David was willing to fight Goliath, and Saul said he could certainly try if he wanted to and offered him his best armor. David refused the armor, as it was so heavy, and said he'd manage better without.

So David went out with his slingshot in one hand. He picked up five nice smooth stones in the other hand and walked toward Goliath.

When Goliath saw him coming, he laughed disdainfully.

"Well, well, well! Look at this now, will you?" he said scornfully. "A baby! Is this all you can find to come and fight me? A boy? I declare, I could die laughing. What a delicious joke! Come on, boy. You'll soon be lunch for bears."

And he flung back his head, laughing and laughing.

"As a matter of fact, it is you who will be lunch for bears, not me, you know," said David. "God is on my side, so look out."

So saying, David put one of his stones in his slingshot and slung it at Goliath. It hit him on the forehead, and he fell down flat on his face, dead.

"There you are, you see," said David. "What did I tell you? Size isn't everything, after all, and God was on my side. Now I really need a sword to cut his head off, but I haven't got one, so I'll cut it off with his own sword."

So David took Goliath's sword and chopped the giant's head off. And when the Philistines saw that their champion was dead, they all ran away and the Israelites ran after them.

Saul was very grateful to David and said he could marry one of his daughters, called Michal.

Soon afterward Samuel died, and everyone was sorry.

The Wisdom of Solomon

After a few more years Saul died, and David became king. Somehow he never quite lived up to his early promise. He was fairly attentive to God's instructions, and he won a lot of battles, and he began to build the city of Jerusalem. But he also did some rather reprehensible things, such as sending a man called Uriah into the front line of a battle to get killed because David wanted to marry Uriah's wife. This was not a good thing at all and God didn't like it. Anyway, David eventually died and his son Solomon became king.

Solomon was an excellent king and got on very well with God. One night God came and talked to Solomon in a dream and said, "Ask what I shall give thee."

"Oh my goodness, what a very difficult question," said Solomon. "There are lots of things I need really; but since I have now become king of this great multitude of people, I should think what I most need is a wise and understanding heart, so that I can judge the people well."

God was delighted with the answer and said that he would be wiser than anyone before him, and no one wiser would come after him.

"What's more," added God, "since you didn't ask for greedy things like riches and fame, I will give them to you as well. And if you keep my commandments, I'll see that you live for a long time."

So Solomon became wise and famous and rich, but most particularly he grew wise. Once when he was in the temple in Jerusalem, overseeing the building that was being done, two women came up to him. They were very angry and were arguing fiercely.

"Now, now," said Solomon. "What is the matter?"

"This is the matter, O King," said one furious woman. (In the old days it was considered extra polite to say "O" before people's names, especially kings. It sounds a bit funny to us, but you get used to it quite soon.)

"This is the matter. This woman and I share an apartment, and we both had baby boys. But the other night this woman's baby died, and when she saw that it was dead, she switched babies and gave me the dead baby while I was still asleep, and took my live baby. I want my baby back again, and she won't give it to me."

"The wretch is lying," screeched the other woman. "The live baby is mine, so why should I give it to her, O King?"

"No it's not. The live baby is mine, O King," said the first woman.

"No it's not."

"Yes it is."

"No it's not."

"Oh, stop arguing," said Solomon, and he called to a servant, "Servant, please go and fetch me a sword."

"Yes, certainly, O King," said the servant, and he fetched a sword.

"What are you going to do with a sword?" asked the servant as he gave it to the king.

"Well," said Solomon. "Since these argumentative women can't agree about who owns the live baby, I shall chop it in half and give the foolish females half each."

This sounds like a very cruel plan and not a bit wise. But it *was* wise, as you will see.

"Oh, what a splendid scheme," said one woman. "By all means chop the baby in two and give us half each. Very fair. How wise you are, O King."

But the other woman became quite distraught.

"Oh no. Oh no, that's a dreadful idea," she said. "Don't do that. Don't cut the baby. I won't argue any more. I'll let her have the baby. I promise I will. I'll do *any*thing so long as you don't chop the baby in half.

Then Solomon said, "Give her the living child and in no way slay it, for she is the mother thereof. No mother would agree to chop up her own baby, so that's how I know whose it is."

So the baby was given to its real mother, and the women went away. It seems unlikely that they shared an apartment much longer.

Solomon reigned long and wisely. He did a great deal of building, particularly in Jerusalem, where he built a beautiful temple. People came from far and wide to hear his wisdom and see his buildings. His most famous visitor was the Queen of Sheba, who could scarcely believe her ears and eyes. Solomon gave her a lot of presents to take home. In his spare time Solomon wrote a rather famous song, appropriately called the "Song of Solomon." He reigned for forty years and then died.

Elijah and the Widow

After Solomon, the Israelites had a variety of kings, most of them fairly awful. The next one worthy of note was called Ahab, and we note him because he was so appallingly wicked. He was the worst of the lot — which is saying something. He paid no attention whatsoever to God or to the commandments. In fact he built altars to Baal everywhere. In fact, Ahab did more to provoke the Lord God of Israel to anger than all the kings of Israel before him.

There was, in the days of Ahab, a wise and holy man of God called Elijah. And God sent Elijah to Ahab with a message. Elijah said to Ahab, "God says that unless you mend your ways, there will be trouble. There won't be any rain or even dew in the country until I say so, and I won't say so until you behave and do what God says."

This made Ahab simply furious.

"How ridiculous," he said. "Who gives a fig about that God any more these days? I couldn't be less interested. Now get out of my sight, you unattractive old man, or you'll be in trouble."

So Elijah hurried away to hide in safety by a brook called Cherith. He drank water from the brook, and God made some large black birds called ravens bring him bread and meat twice a day in their beaks. So he was safe and well cared for.

And there was no rain or dew in the land, and no sign that Ahab cared.

After a while, however, the brook dried up. So God told Elijah to go to a town called Zarephath.

"There's a widow there who will look after you," said God.

So Elijah went to Zarephath and waited outside the gates of the city. As he waited, along came a woman picking up sticks, and Elijah said to her, "Could you please bring me some water to drink and a little cake?"

"Well I haven't got any cake," said the woman. "I'm very short of everything because there's been no rain. In fact, I am just getting a couple of sticks so that I can make a fire. Then I shall use my last dregs of flour and final drip of oil to make a cake for me and my son. Then when we've eaten it, we'll die."

"Oh, but don't worry," said Elijah. "God says that your flour and oil won't run out until after it rains, so that you can look after me."

"Goodness, that doesn't sound very probable to me," said the woman. "But if you want to come and share our last supper, I suppose you can."

Of course, it was just as Elijah had said. The flour and oil never did run out, so she was able to look after him.

But what did happen after a while was that the widow's son fell ill. He was so sick, in fact, that she thought he was dead, and she went to Elijah in a state.

"What have you done this for, you man of God?" she demanded. "Why didn't you let us both die in peace in the first place instead of saving us and letting my son die now? Is this some sort of punishment for my past sins or what?"

Elijah said, "Give the boy to me, and I'll see what can be done."

So Elijah carried the boy up to his loft room and said to God, "Why did you do this to the poor woman after she's looked after me so nicely? It does seem a trifle unfair."

Then he prayed over the boy three times, and the boy got better. Elijah took him back to the widow and said, "See? Here he is. He's perfectly all right now."

"Oh, thank you very much," said the woman. "That's lovely. I always felt fairly sure you were a man of God, and now I know you are without any doubt at all."

Elijah and Ahab

fter about three years without rain, God, said to Elijah: "It's time to deal with Ahab now, because I really want to let it rain."

At the same moment Ahab sent for one of his governors, called Obadiah, and said, "Go all over everywhere, will you, and see if you can find any sign of water anywhere. The horses and mules are dying of thirst. This drought is really maddening."

So Obadiah set off to look in one direction while Ahab set off in another. Obadiah was not one of the Israelites who prayed to Baal. He was one of the few who feared God and kept His commandments. Therefore he was delighted when he happened to meet Elijah.

"Oh Elijah," he said. "How are you? Are you all right? We haven't seen you for a very long time."

"Yes indeed, I am perfectly all right," replied Elijah, "and I would be most grateful if you will please go and tell Ahab that I am here and would like to see him?"

Obadiah was not quite so delighted.

"But good gracious," he said. "Don't you realize that Ahab will almost certainly slay me if I say that? Don't you know that he's been looking for you high and low for ages and has not found you? And now you say 'Go and tell Ahab Elijah's here.' Ten to one by the time I get back here with Ahab, God will have spirited you off somewhere quite else and we won't be able to find you. Then Ahab'll kill me."

"Oh, don't worry," said Elijah. "I promise I'll stay right here. I've got to see Ahab."

So Obadiah calmed down and went to get Ahab. When Ahab saw Elijah he said, "Art thou he that troubleth Israel?"

"No, no," said Elijah. "I have not troubled Israel. You have. You have not kept God's commandments and you've been praying to Baal. Well, now it's time to have a competition between your false gods and my real God. So go and get the Children of Israel and the four hundred and fifty prophets of Baal and meet me at Mount Carmel, and we'll have a simple little test."

So Ahab got the Children of Israel and the prophets of Baal and came to Mount Carmel. And Elijah said to all the people, "Why don't we come to a decision, once and for all. If God is God, follow Him. If Baal is God, follow him."

No one said a word. Not a soul spoke up and said, "Oh, of course God is God." There was just silence.

Then Elijah said, "I, only I, am a prophet of the Lord. But Baal has four hundred and fifty prophets. So here's the plan. I'll prepare wood for a fire, and the prophets of Baal can prepare wood for a fire. They can put some steak on their firewood, ready to be cooked, and I'll put some steak on mine. Then the people who pray to Baal can call on him, and I'll call to God, and whichever god sends fire to cook the steak shall be the real god."

Then all the people said, "That's a frightfully good idea."

So Elijah let the prophets of Baal have the first turn. They built up the dry wood and put the raw meat on top. Then all morning long they shouted for Baal, saying, "Hear us, O Baal!"

But there was no answer. So at about noon Elijah said, mockingly, "Why not shout louder? Perhaps Baal's talking or perhaps he's taking a journey. Or peradventure he's sleeping and needs to be woken up."

So they all shouted their loudest and called for Baal until evening. Then Elijah said, "It's my turn now."

And he built an altar with twelve stones, one for each of the twelve tribes of Israel, and on the top he put wood, and on the top of the wood he put the beef. Then he poured four barrels of water on top of it all, which must have seemed rather wasteful when they were so short, but everyone knows how hard it is to make wet wood burn, and Elijah probably wanted there to be no doubt about God's power.

Then Elijah prayed, "Lord God of Abraham, Isaac and Israel, let it be known this day that you're the real God."

Then at once fire came and burned up everything — meat, wood and stones! And the people fell on their faces and said, "The Lord is God. The Lord is God."

Then they slew all four hundred and fifty of the prophets of Baal.

And Elijah said to Ahab, "You had better have your supper now. I am going up the mountain to pray for some rain."

So Ahab started his supper and Elijah went up Mount Carmel with his servant. Elijah said to his servant, "While I pray, please go and take a look out to sea and tell me what you can see there."

So the servant went and looked and came back and said, "There is nothing."

Elijah sent him to look again and again. Seven times he sent him, and on the seventh time the servant said, "Now I can see a tiny weeny cloud about the size of a man's hand."

"Oh good," said Elijah. "Go down, then, to Ahab and tell him to hurry up with his supper and get into his chariot and rush home. Otherwise he'll get caught in the rain."

So Ahab raced off home in his chariot while huge great thunder clouds seemed to come up from nowhere, and a howling gale began roaring around.

And then came great rain.

Do you think Ahab was grateful and prayed to God? No, he wasn't. He was very angry, and so was his wife, Jezebel. Ahab would have killed Elijah if he'd dared. As it was, he went on being wicked, and God and Elijah were both most disappointed.

Ahab and Naboth

This is the story of one of the wicked things Ahab did. Next door to Ahab's palace was a lovely vineyard. A vineyard, of course, is a place where grapes are grown so that wine may be made. This vineyard belonged to a man called Naboth, who loved it and took enormous care of it because it had belonged to his family for generations.

One day as he was going to his vineyard, Naboth met Ahab.

"Good morning, O King," said Naboth.

"Oh hello, Naboth," said Ahab. "You're just the very person I wanted to see. Would you give me your vineyard please, because it's very near my palace and I'd like to make it into an herb garden. I'll give you lots of money for it and a much better vineyard."

But Naboth said, "Oh goodness, no. I'm afraid I couldn't possibly do that. God forbid! This vineyard has been in my family for ages. It's simply not for sale, I am sorry to say."

Then Ahab behaved exactly like a spoiled child. He went and lay down on his bed and sulked. He turned his face to the wall and refused to eat anything! His wife, Jezebel, who was also very wicked, said to him, "My dear Ahab, whatever's the matter with you? Why aren't you eating and drinking and being happy?"

"Because I'm miserable, that's why," answered Ahab. "That mean Naboth won't let me have his vineyard, the one I want to make into an herb garden. I offered him lots of money for it *and* another vineyard, but he just said 'No.' I *want* his vineyard, I *want* it."

Can you see which commandment he is breaking? Now Jezebel helps him to break several more.

"Well, good heavens," she said to him. "Who's the king here? You or Naboth? Come on, get up and have your supper, and stop being so gloomy. I've thought of an excellent scheme to get Naboth's vineyard for you without paying a penny."

So Jezebel wrote letters for Ahab to seal, and they sent them off to the elders of the city where Naboth lived. The elders of a city were the people who ran it. They were presumably supposed to be old enough to know what was right.

The letters Jezebel wrote said, "Please have a feast in your city and put Naboth to sit in a most important place where everyone can see him. Then find a couple of men who will come in and swear that they heard Naboth blaspheme against God and the king, and then see that they take Naboth out and stone him to death."

Blaspheming is saying evil, untrue things about anything or anyone holy.

Either these elders didn't care about the truth or they were dreadfully scared of Ahab and Jezebel. Whatever the reason, they did exactly what the letters told them to do. They had a feast and put Naboth in an important seat. They found two men who came and bore false witness against Naboth and said they had heard him blaspheme. So then Naboth was taken out of the city, and everyone threw stones at him until he was dead, because they were all stupid enough to believe the liars or else too scared to stand up for Naboth.

Then they sent a message to Jezebel saying that Naboth was dead, and Jezebel said to Ahab, "See? It was simple. Naboth's dead, so now you can have his vineyard without paying for it."

"Oh good," said Ahab. "I'll go and take a walk there right now."

So Ahab went happily off to think about his new herb garden in Naboth's vineyard. But God said to Elijah, "Go down to Ahab in Naboth's vineyard, and tell him that this time he's gone too far, and I've had enough of him."

So Elijah met Ahab in Naboth's vineyard, and Ahab wasn't the least glad to see him.

"Hast thou found me, O mine enemy?" he said to Elijah.

"Yes," said Elijah. "I've found you. I've come because you've been so evil that God is fed up. He says you and all your family will be killed in battle."

And three years later there was war with Syria, and some unknown man "drew a bow at a venture," which means he wasn't really aiming anywhere special; but his arrow killed Ahab. His city was captured too, and Jezebel killed. Their son, Ahaziah, became king for only a short time. He did evil in the sight of the Lord, and then one day he fell out of a window and died.

Elisha

Elijah had grown pretty old by now, so God took him up into heaven one day in a chariot of fire blown up by a whirlwind. Elijah's mantle fell upon a young prophet called Elisha, who took over Elijah's job. Elisha lived in a little house in Samaria with his servant Gehazi. But they did a great deal of traveling — on foot or by donkey — from one place to another, telling people what God was saying.

One of the places they frequently went to was a town called Shunem, where there lived a rich woman and her husband. Every time the rich woman heard that Elisha was in the neighborhood, she invited him to lunch. They were very kind people, and one day the woman said to her husband, "Look, husband, I think that Elisha's a very holy man of God, and as he's continually coming through Shunem, why don't we build him a little room all his own? We can put a bed in it and a table and a stool and a candlestick, so that any time he's here, he can go into his own room and really rest and relax."

"Well, what an excellent thought," said her husband. "Why don't you arrange it?"

So the rich woman arranged it, and when next Elisha came through Shunem, he found a lovely little room all ready for him. He was delighted and said to Gehazi, his servant, "Look, Gehazi, at this perfectly charming room these kind people have made for me. Would you go to the woman and ask her if there's any little thing I can do for her? Would she like an invitation to the king or something?"

So Gehazi asked the woman and came back to Elisha and said, "She says she's perfectly happy, thank you; but as a matter of fact, I happen to know that she would really love to have a son, because she hasn't got any children."

"Oh, really?" said Elisha. "Well, ask her to come here a minute."

So the Shunammite woman stood in Elisha's doorway, and Elisha said, "By this time next year you'll have a baby boy."

"Oh! That will be lovely," said the woman. "I only hope you're not joking."

Of course Elisha wasn't joking. She did have a baby boy and she was delighted. But a few years later the little boy was out in the fields with his father watching the reapers when he got a dreadful headache.

"Oh my head, my head," he said.

So they took him back to his mother, who put him on her lap. But he died. Immediately his mother thought of Elisha, and, getting on a donkey, she raced as fast as the donkey could go to Mount Carmel, where Elisha was. She told Elisha the whole story, and Elisha said he'd come at once. But he sent Gehazi hurrying on ahead.

"Take my staff, Gehazi," he said, "and lay it on the boy's face in case it helps. And don't stop on the way to talk or eat or sleep or anything."

So Gehazi rushed off, closely followed by Elisha and the boy's mother.

Gehazi got there first, of course, and put Elisha's staff on the boy's face. But it did no good, so he went back to meet Elisha, who was just arriving.

"It didn't do any good," said Gehazi. "The child didn't wake up."

Then Elisha went into the boy's room and shut the door. The boy was lying on the bed looking rather dead. So Elisha prayed to God and then put his mouth on the boy's mouth and his body on the boy's body. The boy's body grew warm, and he sneezed seven times and opened his eyes!

Elisha took the boy back to his mother, and no doubt he grew up to be a comfort to his parents in their old age, because that's what children used to do.

Elisha and Naaman

The king of Syria, who fought on and off against the Israelites, had a favorite captain in his army. The captain was called Naaman, and he was an excellent soldier, brave and strong and honorable. Naaman had a wife, and when he captured an Israelite girl in battle, he gave her to his wife to be her maid. Naaman also had a dread disease called leprosy. Leprosy makes your flesh go all white and unhealthy, and then your fingers eventually drop off and it's not a bit pleasant.

Although she had been captured and taken from her home, the little Israelite maid was extremely fond of Naaman and Naaman's wife, and was quite upset when Naaman got leprosy. Naturally, Naaman's wife was upset, too, and one day she was talking to her maid about it.

"Poor Naaman," she said. "He's getting so depressed about his leprosy. It really is rather trying for him. I wish I could do something about it."

"Oh I know," said the maid. "I've been thinking about it quite a lot, too, and I really wish he'd go to Samaria to see the holy man of God. I'm sure he could cure leprosy."

"Oh really?" said Naaman's wife. "What is the man's name? Tell me more about this. Perhaps we could arrange something."

"He's called Elisha," said the maid, "and he's one of my people and very holy."

Then someone happened to mention it to Naaman.

"Look," they said. "Thus and thus said the little maid from the land of Israel."

So Naaman went to the king of Syria to ask for leave to go and get his leprosy cured by the Israelite prophet.

"Oh yes, of course, of course," said the king of Syria. "Go, and good luck go with you. I'll write a letter saying you've come to be cured, and you can take it with you."

So Naaman took the letter from the king of Syria. He also took six thousand pieces of gold, ten pieces of silver and ten sets of new clothes as a reward to be given when he was cured. We don't know how large the pieces of gold were; but even if they were tiny, six thousand of them would make it quite an expensive cure. But worth it, because at that time leprosy was seldom curable.

For some unknown reason the king of Syria had addressed his letter to the king of Israel rather than to Elisha, so of course Naaman went to the king of Israel and gave him the letter. When the king of Israel read the letter, he was fearfully upset and ripped his clothes.

"Does the king of Syria think I am God or something?" he asked. "How does he think I can cure diseases? He is just trying to pick a quarrel so that he can fight us again. Oh dear. Oh dear, what a beastly worry."

But when Elisha heard that the king of Israel was ripping his clothes because he couldn't cure diseases, Elisha sent a message to the king saying, "Don't rip your clothes. It's me that Naaman should be coming to, not you. Send him on to me."

So with a sigh of relief the king of Israel sent Naaman on to Elisha, with all his gold and silver and clothes. Gehazi went to the door to meet him.

"Good afternoon," said Gehazi. "What can I do for you?"

"Oh," said Naaman. "I've been sent by the king of Syria to see if Elisha can cure my leprosy."

"Well, wait a minute," said Gehazi. "I'll just go and ask my master."

A moment later Gehazi came back with a message from Elisha.

"My master says that you are to go and wash seven times in the river Jordan, and then you'll be better. Your leprosy will go away."

Surprisingly enough, Naaman was furious. For one thing, he was not used to being given messages by servants. For another, he thought the cure was silly and unspectacular.

"What?" he said angrily. "D'you mean he's not even going to bother to come to see me himself? He's not going to pray over me, or hit me with his staff, or do any of the usual things? You mean I've got to take instructions from a mere servant? Really, it's too disgraceful. And anyway, what's wrong with the rivers of my country, I should like to know? Abana and Pharpar are much better than all the rivers of Israel. How could it possibly make me better to wash in that messy, murky old river Jordan? Honestly! The man is obviously not properly qualified at all. The entire thing is an insult."

And he worked himself into a real rage over it. Finally one of his servants went up to him and said soothingly, "But sir, supposing Elisha had told you to do some very difficult and brave thing, wouldn't you at least have tried? Isn't it much simpler to go and wash in a muddy little river? Why don't you try? It can't do any harm to try, and after all, it might even work. You'll never know if you don't try."

Naaman allowed himself to be mollified and said, "Oh, well, I suppose you're right, but it seems a very silly, dull sort of cure, all the same."

And he went off, muttering, to swim seven times in the Jordan. Needless to say, after the seventh swim, Naaman came out of the river with skin as pink and pure as a baby's. There is obviously something very special about doing things seven times.

Naaman was wild with delight and rushed straight back to Elisha to thank him. This time Elisha did come out to see him.

"I simply cannot thank you enough," said Naaman to Elisha. "Now I know that your God is, indeed, remarkably powerful. Would you like some of this gold and silver and new clothes as a small token of my great gratitude."

"No, indeed, thank you very much," said Elisha. "God did it, after all. I only passed His message on to you. I am extremely glad you are better."

"Well, thanks again," said Naaman, "and from now on I will pray only to your God, not to any other. But do you think He will forgive me if I bow down to the false god Rimmon when I have to go and pray with the king of Syria? I'll be praying to your God, but I'll have to bow to Rimmon or it wouldn't be polite to my king. What do you think?"

"I think it'll be all right," said Elisha. "Go in peace."

So Naaman left. Meanwhile, Elisha's servant, who had been listening, was having some very sinful thoughts.

"Well," he said to himself, "I think it is a big pity not to have taken some of the gold and the clothes from Naaman. It's a waste. They'd come in very handy. I think I'll go secretly after Naaman and get some for myself."

So Gehazi followed after Naaman, and Naaman saw him coming and stopped his chariot.

"Hello there!" called Naaman. "What's the matter? Is everything all right?"

"Oh yes," said Gehazi, "everything's fine, but my master has changed his mind about the gold and the garments and would like some after all."

"Oh, by all means," said Naaman. "Take whatever Elisha wants. He's more than welcome to all of it."

So Gehazi took some clothes and some silver back with him and hid them in his room, and then went in to see Elisha.

Where have you been, Gehazi?" asked Elisha. "What were you doing?"

"Been? Been? I haven't been anywhere, I wasn't doing anything," lied Gehazi.

"You're lying, I'm afraid," said Elisha. "I can tell. I know what you did. You went and took some of the reward from Naaman, didn't you. Well, you shouldn't have. You don't deserve a reward. It's like stealing. So as a punishment I'm afraid you'll have to have Naaman's leprosy."

And Gehazi's skin became white with leprosy.

After this, there were many more kings in Israel, but most of them did evil in the sight of the Lord, and so did the people, except for a few. So when, several centuries later, the king of Babylon came and besieged Jerusalem, the holy city of Israel, God didn't help the Israelites. Jerusalem fell. The temple was completely smashed, and the Ark of the Covenant was wrecked. The king of Babylon took all the valuables out of the temple and out of the city. There was hardly anything left of the city at all. Thousands of Israelites were killed, and thousands more were taken to Babylon to be slaves.

The fall of Jerusalem is the saddest event in the history of the Jewish people. For hundreds of years afterwards, they had no land of their own but were strangers in other people's lands. The only good thing that came of it at the time was that the Jews became much more strong-minded about keeping all the laws of Moses, and about remembering they had only one God to pray to, no matter how many strange gods other people prayed to. And throughout all the following generations, they never lost the hope that they would one day return to Jerusalem, their holy city.

PART THREE

Shadrach, Meshach and Abednego

hen Nebuchadnezzar, the king of Babylon, destroyed Jerusalem, he took all the valuable gold and silver and treasure out of the temple back to Babylon with him.

He also took with him several of the wisest, most intelligent, and best-educated young Jews, in case they might be useful. He sent them to school to learn Chaldean, which was the language they spoke in Babylon. They also learned things like astrology.

Three of these wise Jews saved by Nebuchadnezzar were called Shadrach, Meshach and Abednego. They were so wise that before long the king gave them the most important jobs running the country. The king found they were ten times wiser than his Babylonian politicians. Naturally, this made the Babylonians furiously jealous, and they determined to get rid of the Jews. And Nebuchadnezzar unwittingly played right into their hands.

Nebuchadnezzar built a huge, great golden statue and sent for all his princes, governors, captains, judges, counselors, sheriffs and rulers to come and see it. Then a herald shouted out to them all: "Listen all of you. Whenever you hear music played on the cornet, flute, harp, sackbut, psaltery and dulcimer, you must immediately fall down and pray to this gorgeous golden statue. If you don't instantly stop what you're doing when you hear that music and start praying to this statue, you will be thrown into a burning fiery furnace."

"Hurrah, hurrah! What a good idea," said all the people, because they didn't mind one little bit which statue they prayed to, and had no intention of being flung into a burning fiery furnace.

"Hurrah, hurrah! What a good idea," said the enemies of the three Jews. "Those annoying Jews will never agree to pray to a statue, so they'll be burned. Hurrah!"

The sackbut is an old-fashioned kind of trombone, and the psaltery and dulcimer are both old-fashioned instruments with strings to pluck. People still play the dulcimer sometimes.

Everything went according to plan. Whenever the people heard music from the cornet, flute, harp, sackbut, psaltery and dulcimer, they began at once to pray to the statue, no matter what they might be doing at the moment.

Everyone, that is, except Shadrach, Meshach and Abednego. They paid no attention to the music at all and went right on praying to God.

"Hurrah, hurrah!" said their enemies, rubbing their hands with glee. "We've got them now." And they went straight off to Nebuchadnezzar.

"O King, live forever," they said, which was just their polite way of saying "Good morning" to royalty.

"O King, live forever. Didn't you make a new law that everyone should pray to that statue whenever they heard music on the cornet, flute, harp, et cetera? And that whoever didn't would be burned?"

"Yes, yes," said the king. "I thought it might be a good idea. A break in routine you know. What of it?"

"Well," said the men. "Those three Jews that have the best jobs, they don't pray to the statue at all."

Nebuchadnezzar was simply furious.

"How wicked," he shouted. "Fetch the Jews. Build the fire."

So Shadrach, Meshach and Abednego were brought to the king, who said, "Is it true that you don't pray to my statue? Because if so, you should be burned. But if you do pray to it, the next time you hear all that music on the cornet, flute, harp, sackbut, psaltery and dulcimer, then you'll be all right. Otherwise, you'll be burned, and what god can save you from fire, I should like to know?"

Then Shadrach, Meshach and Abednego said to the king, "We don't even have to stop and think for a minute before answering you. Of course we didn't pray to your statue. What a crazy idea. We pray only to God. We'll never pray to any old statue. We'd far rather be burned. If God wants to rescue us, He will. If not, never mind."

"Well, now, I'm much crosser than ever," said Nebuchadnezzar. "How can you be so idiotically obstinate when you're so clever? I shall make the fire seven times hotter than usual to serve you right."

So then the king ordered the burning fiery furnace to be made seven times hotter, and he commanded the strongest men in his army to tie up Shadrach, Meshach and Abednego and fling them into the raging fire. And because the fire was so fearfully fierce, the strong soldiers were burned to death just from getting close enough to it to throw in the Jews.

Shadrach, Meshach and Abednego fell down into the burning fiery furnace and the king watched. Suddenly he became astonished and then frightened, and said to his counselors in a terrified voice, "Hey, what's going on around here? Didn't we just throw in three men tied up?"

"True, O King," said the counselors. "We most certainly did. Why do you ask?"

"Well, look what I see in the flames," said the king. "Not three men tied up and burning, but four men walking about untied. And the fourth man looks rather like an angel. I'm scared of this."

So then he went as near as he could to the fire and shouted out: "Shadrach, Meshach and Abednego, you can come out now if you like. Obviously your God is extremely powerful after all."

So Shadrach, Meshach and Abednego came out of the fire, and all their enemies saw that they weren't one bit burnt. Their hair wasn't even singed, and their clothes didn't even smell of fire. And Nebuchadnezzar said, "Shadrach, Meshach and Abednego, you are very brave, and any god who sends angels to keep people safe from fire is a pretty strong god. So I'll make a new law: 'Anyone who says anything against your God shall be cut up into ribbons and his house shall be made into a rubbish heap.' And I'll give even grander jobs to you three."

So Shadrach, Meshach and Abednego got even better jobs, which must have made their enemies furious. But their enemies wouldn't dare to say anything, in case they were cut up into ribbons and their houses turned into rubbish heaps.

Nebuchadnezzar's Dream

Another wise Jew that Nebuchadnezzar had saved from Jerusalem was called Daniel. He was at school with Shadrach, Meshach and Abednego, when one night Nebuchadnezzar had a dream that disturbed him. When he awoke in the morning, he was thoroughly worried and sent for all his Babylonian wise men and astrologers to explain his dream to him.

"Good morning, wise men," said the king. "I've had a very troubling dream. Please tell me what it means."

"Why of course, O King," said the wise men. "What was your dream?"

"Gracious, I don't know," said the king. "I've forgotten it completely, but it was very worrying; so if you can't tell me what my dream was and what it means, you can all be cut up into ribbons, and your houses will be turned into rubbish heaps."

He seems to have been a bit unimaginative about his punishments.

"But," he went on, "if you can tell me what I dreamed, and what it means, you can have lots of lovely presents."

"If you don't tell us what you dreamed, O King," said the wise men, "we can't possibly tell you what it means. This is an impossible thing you are asking. No wise man has ever been expected to know such a thing before. No one could possibly tell you what you dreamed."

Then the king got into another furious temper and sent out an order to chop all the wise men into pieces and turn their houses into rubbish heaps if they couldn't tell him his dream.

Fortunately, just in the nick of time, Daniel heard about it from Arioch, the captain of the king's guard.

"What's the great hurry about?" asked Daniel. "If the king gives me a little time, I can probably give him the answer."

So the king agreed not to chop the wise men into ribbons just yet, and Daniel went in and prayed. And God gave him the whole answer in a dream. So Daniel went to Arioch and said, "Never mind about chopping up the wise men. I am going to tell the king his dream now."

Then Arioch said to the king, "Here's one of the captives from Jerusalem. He's going to tell you about your dream."

"Oh good," said Nebuchadnezzar. "Do you know what I dreamed? How clever."

"Well, it wasn't very clever, really," said Daniel. "Our God told me, you see. This is what you dreamed. You dreamed you saw a great big statue with a gold head, silver arms, brass stomach, iron legs and feet of half-iron, half-clay. Then the statue collapsed because a large stone knocked it down. The large stone turned into a mountain, but the bits of the statue all blew away and disappeared."

"Oh, you're absolutely right," said Nebuchadnezzar in amazement. "That's exactly what I dreamed! I remember it all now. So what does it mean?"

"Well, the meaning's rather complicated," said Daniel, "but the general idea is that you've been given a strong kingdom by God — that's the golden head of the statue. After you will come other kingdoms of varying strength — that's the silver, brass and iron part. Last of all, someone stronger than all of them will come and win this kingdom. That is the stone that smashed the statue and then turned into a mountain."

"Oh, thank you very much," said the king. "You Jews really do seem to have a most unusual God."

So he gave Daniel lots of presents as well as the job of chief adviser to the king himself. This was an even grander job than the ones Shadrach, Meshach and Abednego had.

Eventually the dream came true. Nebuchadnezzar went mad and ate grass, and his kingdom was taken over by Belshazzar.

The Writing on the Wall

Belshazzar was Nebuchadnezzar's son, but he seems to have been rather brainless. He gave a great feast one day for a thousand lords and princes and their wives, and after they'd all had a good deal of wine, Belshazzar thought it might be rather fun to have dinner using all the holy plates his father had taken from the temple in Jerusalem. So he ordered his servants to bring out the golden vessels and use them. They drank out of holy golden goblets, ate off holy golden plates and thought it was all most hilarious.

But suddenly, in the middle of their feasting, Belshazzar looked at the wall, and just beside a candlestick he saw a hand appear and write some words on the wall. He was so terrified that his knees knocked together.

"Oh goodness!" he cried. "What's this? What does it mean? Oh, it must be something frightening. Where are all the wise men? Send for them quickly. Whoever can tell me what this writing means shall have lots of scarlet clothes and a gold chain around his neck, and I'll even give him part of my kingdom to rule."

In those days scarlet or purple dye was so difficult and expensive to get that only kings wore scarlet and purple clothes; so it's really not such a dull reward as it sounds.

All the king's wise men came pouring in to look at the writing on the wall because they were all longing to have scarlet clothes and gold chains and a small kingdom. But to no avail. Not one of them could understand what the writing said, and they went back to bed.

Then Belshazzar was so upset and worried and miserable, that his lords were all astonished. And so was the queen, but she proved to be the only person around with any sense.

"O King, live forever," she said. "Why are you so distraught? Why on earth don't you ask Daniel? Your father asked Daniel's advice on just about every problem because he is so wise and his God so powerful. It seems to me only common sense to ask Daniel instead of carrying on like this."

She was perfectly right, of course, but the trouble with common sense is that it is not common at all.

The king calmed down.

"My dear, you're perfectly right," he said. "We'll send for Daniel at once."

So Daniel came and stood before Belshazzar, who said, "Are you the Daniel I've heard so much about? Because if so, I'd be grateful if you'd just explain this curious writing that has appeared from outer space on my wall. If you can, you shall have lots of scarlet clothes and a gold chain and some of my kingdom to rule."

"Oh, you can keep your clothes and rewards, O King," said Daniel. "I really don't want them. But as for this writing, I'll certainly explain it. It is a message from my God, the God of the Jews. It says *Mene Mene Tekel Uphar-sin*, which means that God has weighed you in the balance and found you wanting. He has weighed what you've done against what you should have done, and it does not balance.

"Your father, Nebuchadnezzar, had a great kingdom and was quite a good king," continued Daniel. "But he got too big for his boots, and God was not pleased. So then he went crazy and ate grass.

"You knew all this when you became king; but instead of being a good king, look what you've done — you sat about having wasteful feasts. And worst of all, you've used holy plates and goblets, and that is wicked and just showing off.

"The net result of your silly, lazy ways is that the Medes and Persians will take your kingdom from you because you simply don't deserve it."

Belshazzar was so unnerved by the entire incident that he believed every word Daniel said and gave him some red clothes and a gold chain willy-nilly.

And in any event, Daniel was absolutely right because that very night the Medes attacked. Belshazzar was killed, and Darius, the king of the Medes, took over the kingdom.

Daniel and the Lions' Den

Darius was a good king, and he made Daniel the chief ruler in the country. He told all the princes and presidents and judges to account to Daniel for everything. So of course they were all horribly jealous of Daniel and made plots to get rid of him. But it was very difficult, because Daniel was so wise and fair and honorable and just. This merely made his enemies more jealous and more mean.

"Really, this Daniel is too much. Imagine having to account to him for everything," they said. "It's going too far. We can't even cheat on our taxes without him noticing. It's too much. Why, he's only a foreigner, and a Jew at that. What can we do to get rid of him?"

"Well, as he doesn't do anything wrong, we will have to trick him somehow," said others.

"Ha! I've the very thing," said one. "Here's an excellent trick. Let's get the king to say that no one must ask any god for anything for thirty days. Daniel is sure to go on praying to his God three times a day. The Jews all do. Then we'll catch him."

"Oh, how clever," they said. "That's a terrific plot. What shall the punishment be for those who disobey?

"How about throwing them into the lions' den to be eaten up? Would that be a good idea?"

"The very thing," they all agreed.

So the princes and presidents went to Darius and said, "O King, live forever. We've all consulted together and we would like you to make a decree that for thirty days no one is to ask any god or any man for anything, and if they do, O King, then they can be cast into a den of lions for punishment."

Darius never saw the plot and agreed quite amicably to sign the decree.

All went exactly as the plotters had plotted. Daniel paid no attention whatever to such a silly law. He went on praying three times a day to God by his window facing toward Jerusalem, exactly as he always did.

Gleefully the plotters went to Darius and said, "By the way, O King, Daniel the Jew doesn't pay any attention to your new law. He is still asking his God for things three times a day."

Then, too late, Darius saw the plot against his friend Daniel and was most miserable. He argued with the men until nightfall, trying to save Daniel. But it was useless.

"No, no," said the wicked men happily. "You know perfectly well, O King, that no law of the Medes and Persians may ever be changed."

So Daniel was brought to Darius, and Darius was horribly unhappy.

"Oh, Daniel," he said. "I am so very sorry about this. It was a most dastardly plot, and there's nought I can do about it. I'm afraid you'll just have to be thrown into the lions' den. I only hope to goodness that your God will save you, though I can't imagine how He could."

"Don't worry, O King," said Daniel.

Then was Daniel cast into the den of lions, and the way out was sealed up with the king's own seal so that there was no chance for Daniel to escape.

His enemies went cheerfully home.

"That's cooked his goose," they said.

Darius went sorrowfully home and had a most wretched night. His servants tried all they could to cheer him up.

"Would you like your dinner now, O King?" they asked.

"What?" asked Darius. "Eat dinner while my best friend is being lions' dinner? I couldn't eat a thing. Take it away."

They tried again.

"Would you like us to play you some soothing music, O King?" they asked.

"Soothing music?" replied Darius. "Can't you see how miserable I am? How can I listen to music when Daniel is probably already dead? Leave me alone, for heaven's sake."

The night eventually passed and day dawned. The unhappy king hurried hopelessly to the lions' den and shouted through the door, "Oh Daniel, Daniel. Was your God strong enough to save you, or are you dead?"

Imagine how his heart leapt with joy when he heard Daniel's voice calmly saying, "O King, live forever. I am perfectly all right, thank you. God sent an angel to shut the lions' mouths and sheath their claws, and I had a thoroughly peaceful night."

"Oh, thank goodness," said Darius. "I was *so* worried and unhappy."

Then Daniel was taken out of the lions' den, and all the wicked plotters and their families were flung in instead. And the lions gobbled them up, thankfully.

"I shall make a new law now," said Darius to Daniel. "Everyone in my kingdom shall fear your God, because He is the living God and remarkably strong."

So Daniel prospered while Darius was king. After Darius came Cyrus, a Persian king, who liked Daniel, too.

Daniel and Bel

In the days of King Cyrus, the Babylonians had an idol, or holy statue, called Bel. Everyone, including Cyrus, went daily to worship it. Every day people brought the idol twelve measures of the best flour, forty sheep and six vessels of wine for the idol to eat and drink. Every day!

Cyrus went to pray to this statue, but of course Daniel didn't. Daniel prayed to his own God, the God of Abraham, Isaac and Jacob. So one day Cyrus said to Daniel, "Oh Daniel, I've been meaning to ask you, why don't you come and worship Bel?"

"You must be joking," said Daniel. "I don't worship lifeless old statues made by men out of brass or clay or gold or anything. I pray only to the living God, who has made heaven and earth and everything in them. Pray to a statue? Goodness, I should think not."

"Oh, but why do you say Bel isn't a living god?" asked Cyrus. "Don't you know how much he eats and drinks every day?"

Then Daniel smiled and said, "You mustn't be too easily deceived, O King. This Bel of yours is clay inside and brass outside, and has never eaten or drunk a single thing ever. It's just a lifeless statue."

Then Cyrus was furious that he might be being tricked, and he sent for all the priests of Bel, of whom there were no fewer than seventy, and their families.

And Cyrus said, "Now then. If you don't immediately tell me who is eating all these twelve measures of flour and forty sheep every day and drinking all that wine, you'll all jolly well die at once.

"On the other hand, if you can prove to me that Bel eats and drinks it all, then Daniel can certainly die for saying it's only a statue because that would be blasphemy if Bel's really a god."

And Daniel said, "Yes, O King. I quite agree with that. Now let's all go to Bel's temple and set everything up."

So off went Cyrus and Daniel and the seventy priests with their families to the temple. And the priests said, "All right, O King, now we'll go out, and you and Daniel can put the flour and meat and wine in here for Bel to devour. Then you can shut up the temple and seal it with your own seal, so that no one can get in or out. And in the morning, if Bel hasn't eaten it all, well, we'll die. But he surely will have eaten it up, so Daniel will die."

Then the priests all left, and they didn't seem a bit worried. But then Daniel didn't seem a bit worried either.

"Come on, O King," he said. "Put the food on the table. But before you seal the place up, do you mind if my servants sprinkle some ash all over the floor?"

"No, no, of course not. Do whatever you like," said Cyrus.

So Daniel's servants sprinkled a light covering of ash all over the temple floor, then the place was locked up and sealed with the king's seal.

But in the middle of the night, through a secret entrance came the seventy priests with their wives and children. And they ate up all the food and drank up all the wine, as they did every night. They were as happy as anything, thinking that they had caught Daniel at last! But they never noticed the smooth covering of ash on the floor.

Then in the morning betime — which means early — the king got up and Daniel, too, and they went together to the temple.

"What about the seals, Daniel?" asked the king. "Are they whole?"

"Oh yes, rather," said Daniel. "They're whole all right."

So the door was opened, and they looked in and what did they see? All the food gone, of course, and the table bare.

"O Bel, you didn't trick me after all," said Cyrus, who didn't much like the idea that he had been wasting his prayers on a lump of clay. "You're not just a silly statue. You are a living god."

But Daniel smiled and held on to the king and said, "Don't go in, O King. Take a look at the floor where my servants put all that smooth ash. What can you see there?"

The king looked, and was aghast.

"Good heavens, you're perfectly right. I can see the footprints of men, women, and children. It's those greedy, deceitful priests. They tricked me. Bel *is* only a silly statue after all. Where are those priests? I'll slay them."

Then the king was furiously angry. He and Daniel found the secret entranceway, and the whole trick became clear to the king. He slew all the seventy priests and all their families, and Daniel broke up the statue of Bel and destroyed the temple.

Daniel and the Dragon

Y ou would think that by now the king and the Babylonians would have given up praying to silly things. But not so. Now that Bel was broken, there was a great big dragon to whom they all prayed. We don't know what sort of dragon it was, but probably it was some kind of crocodile. Anyway, it was most certainly alive!

So Cyrus said to Daniel, "Now you can't say that this is only a brass god. He is definitely alive, and he eats and drinks. He is a living god, so come and worship him with me."

"No, no, O King," said Daniel. "I worship only the living God that no one can kill and who won't die. This old dragon, now, he'll die one day. In fact, if you'll let me, I could easily kill this dragon without even a sword or any weapon."

The king said, "All right. Try. I'll let you."

So Daniel took some pitch and fat and hair, and boiled it all up together into a gummy mess and made lumps out of it for the dragon to eat. The dragon took it in his mouth, couldn't eat it properly and popped!

"See?" said Daniel. "This is the useless sort of god you pray to — a dragon so stupid that it eats lumps of inedible glue and then pops."

The king agreed with Daniel, but the Babylonians were all very angry and got together in a crowd.

"Look what's happening," they said enraged. "Our king is positively turning into a Jew because of Daniel. First he destroys Bel and kills the priests. Now he's slain our dragon. We must do something about this before things get any worse."

What they did was to go to the king and threaten him.

"Come on," they said angrily. "You'd better hand Daniel over to us at once. We've had enough of him and his God. If you don't give him to us, we'll destroy you and your house, so make up your mind."

There were so many of them, and they were so threatening, that Cyrus at last had to agree. He gave Daniel to them, and they flung him, once again, into a den of lions. There were seven lions in this den, and they usually ate several sheep every day. In order to make them extra hungry for Daniel, they weren't given any sheep to eat that day. And Daniel didn't get anything to eat, either.

Now miles away, out in the country, there lived a man called Habakkuk. He had just made an enormous stew and was about to take it out to the men who were harvesting in the fields.

What was his amazement, then, when an angel said to him suddenly, out of the blue, "Oh, Habakkuk, God says will you please take that stew to Babylon and give it to Daniel, who is in the lions' den."

"B . . . b . . . but I can't," gasped poor Habakkuk. "I've never been to Babylon. I don't even know where it is, so how could I find the city, let alone the lions' den?"

"Oh really, I do wish people wouldn't always argue so," said the angel, and he picked up Habakkuk by the hair of his head and carried him, stew and all, through the air, over the countryside, and put him down on a rock overlooking the lions' den!

Poor Habakkuk, he must have been a bit surprised and breathless, but anyway he shouted out, "Hey, Daniel, Daniel, come here and get the dinner God sent you."

"Oh thank you. How kind of you and how marvelous of God," said Daniel. And he took the dinner from Habakkuk. Then Habakkuk was wafted back to his home again, where presumably he had to make another lunch for the men who were harvesting.

Meanwhile, Daniel cheerfully ate the stew and let us hope he shared it with the lions, who were so kindly not eating him.

On the seventh day Cyrus came to the den to bewail his friend Daniel, but behold! When he looked in, there was Daniel cheerfully sitting with the friendly lions.

Then the king said very loudly, "Oh Daniel, I am so happy to see you alive. Your God really is a truly great God. There's none other like Him, I must agree."

So he took Daniel out of the den and flung all his enemies in instead. And they were all eaten up in a trice.

Jonah and the Whale

O ne day God sent a message to a man named Jonah.

"Get up, Jonah," said God. "Go to that great big city of Nineveh and warn them there that I'm tired of their wickedness and am thinking of destroying the city."

But Jonah didn't want to go.

"Oh help," he said to himself. "Nineveh's the last place I want to go to. I think I'll go somewhere else for a while and get away from God. I'll pretend I never heard what He said."

So he found a ship going to Tarshish, paid his fare, and set off to get away from God. But of course God knew just what was going on, and He sent a great storm where the ship was sailing. The sailors were all terrified by the storm. They flung out all their heavy belongings to keep the ship from sinking, they prayed to all their various gods, but still the storm went on.

Jonah, however, was sleeping peacefully through all the roaring and raging until the captain came and woke him up.

"What on earth do you think you are doing there fast asleep?" the captain said crossly to Jonah. "Wake up and pray to your God in case He can stop this storm before we all drown."

Then all the sailors got together and said, "Let's cast lots to see whose fault this storm is."

Casting lots is like saying "Eenie, meenie, minie, mo." So they cast lots and it fell on Jonah.

"This storm seems to be your fault," they said to Jonah. "Who are you and what are you doing here?"

"Well, I'm a Jew," said Jonah, "and I'm running away from God because I didn't like the instructions He gave me."

Then the men were scared because they had heard how powerful the Jew's God was.

"What do you think we had better do?" they asked Jonah.

"I suppose you had better throw me into the sea," answered Jonah bravely. "Then the storm will probably stop because I'm afraid it probably *is* my fault."

The sailors didn't want to do this because they were kind, and they tried all they could to save the ship and Jonah. But to no avail. So in the end they threw Jonah overboard and instantly the sea grew calm! The sailors were awestruck.

Jonah, of course, was expecting to drown, but God had quite different ideas on the subject. After all, Jonah hadn't yet delivered the message God had given him. So at the precise moment that Jonah fell into the sea, God caused a gigantic fish, with its huge jaws wide open to catch some lunch, to go cruising by the ship. Jonah fell right into the enormous creature's giant jaws and was swallowed whole! He must have been quite surprised by his new and unexpected surroundings, but he probably preferred them to being drowned. He spent three days in the fish's belly, most of the time deciding that it was a waste of time trying to escape from God since it was obviously impossible. He told God he would certainly deliver His message for him, and said he was sorry for pretending not to hear it.

So on the third day the fish decided it had had enough of this uncomfortable obstruction in its belly, and it burped Jonah up — fortunately on dry land.

"Are you sure you are going to Nineveh now?" asked God when Jonah got his breath back.

"Oh definitely," said Jonah, and he set off at once on the three days' journey to the wicked great city.

"Listen to me, all you awful people," he said when he got there. "In forty days God is going to wreck this place if you don't behave better."

Then absolutely everyone in Nineveh was worried and sorry. They all ripped their clothes and wore sackcloth and ashes. The king ordered everyone to fast, which is the opposite of feast, and to pray to God and to stop being violent.

"If God sees we're really sorry," said the king, "perhaps he won't wreck our city."

And God did change his mind because they were sorry. But somehow Jonah didn't seem to realize this, and he was cross.

"Well, for heaven's sake, God," he said. "What's the point of all this? Here I am hanging around the city for forty days waiting for all that destruction, and it never comes. Now I look a perfect fool."

God decided Jonah needed to learn some sense, and He thought an object lesson might be better than words. Jonah was sitting outside the city by a little fence, and as it was very hot in the sun, God caused a gourd to grow up to shelter Jonah from the heat. Jonah was very grateful; but when God sent a worm to eat up the plant, Jonah became peevish again.

"Look here," said God. "Do you think you are right to be annoyed about the gourd?"

"Well, yes, I certainly do," answered Jonah. "I mean to say, what a fearful waste of the gourd's time growing if it's just going to be eaten by some dismal grub."

"Well there you are," said God. "You're all muddled. You think I should not have destroyed the gourd, which took only a day to grow. Yet you think I ought to destroy the whole of the city of Nineveh, which took ages to build and, what's more, is full of thousands of people and children and even animals, who all took years to grow."

The Story of Esther

Now, another king who once gave a great feast was King Ahasuerus. He was king of a good deal of the country between India and Ethiopia. He wanted to show off to all the neighboring kings how grand and rich and important he was. The kings of Persia and Media were among those invited to the feast. They were invited to stay for a hundred and eighty days, which is about six months, and at the end of that time, there were seven days of feasting. So you can see that this was no spur-of-the-moment weekend party! The decorations in the garden were white, green, blue and purple. The beds were of gold and silver, and the floors were of red, blue, white and black marble. Quite jolly!

They all drank from golden vessels, each one different, but no one had to drink who didn't want to. This was the king's special rule, because it was usually considered exceedingly rude not to drink everything you were given. It could even cause small wars!

King Ahasuerus had a wife, called Queen Vashti, who had her own palace on the grounds, and she gave her own feast for the other queens and wives. (Women weren't considered of much account in those days and seldom feasted with their husbands. They probably had a more amusing time.) But Queen Vashti was very, very beautiful, so on the seventh day of feasting, when the king was feeling thoroughly merry, he decided to send for Vashti so that all the other princes could see how beautiful she was and be envious. The queen, however, had no wish to be gazed at by a lot of over-merry monarchs, so she refused to go. This made Ahasuerus furious. And it also made him look like a fool in front of his guests.

So he said to the other kings, "What is your advice? What shall I do to this queen of mine who doesn't obey me? She's put me in a dreadful temper."

"And not only that," said a Persian prince, "she's set a rotten example for all other women to follow. All our wives will say, 'Why should we come when you order us to? Queen Vashti didn't, so we won't.' Then we'll all look like fools, too. You must do something about it at once."

"Well I know that," said Ahasuerus peevishly. "Of course I've got to do something. But what? That's what I want to know."

"Well," said the Persian, "why don't you simply say she won't be queen anymore, and you'll give all her jewels and things to another, more obedient queen? Then when everyone in your huge empire knows this, the wives will be jolly careful to obey their husbands, in case they aren't allowed to be wives any more."

"Oh very sensible," said the king. And he did just that, and everyone in his kingdom was told, and no more was heard of Vashti. Let us hope she was happy not to be a queen any more.

But after all his guests had gone home, Ahasuerus was not so happy. He began to miss Vashti and be lonely, and at last his servants suggested that he really should look for a replacement.

"Send people out all through your kingdom picking out pretty girls," they advised, "and bring them here for you to choose the prettiest. And the girl you like best can be queen instead of Vashti. How's that for a plan?"

"Excellent," said Ahasuerus. "Do it."

Now in the very city of Shushan where the king lived, there also lived a Jew called Mordecai. He had been taken into captivity when Jerusalem fell, and had brought with him his niece, Hadassah, whose parents had been killed. He had brought Hadassah up as his own daughter, and had translated her name to Esther.

Esther had grown up to be a very beautiful maiden, so she was one of the many lovely damsels brought to the palace to be looked at by the king. Mordecai told her not to let on that she was Jewish, so she didn't.

At last the day came for the king to pick the queen. There he sat on his throne, holding a crown ready to put on the new queen, and one by one the lovely maidens came before him, hoping to be picked. But Esther was the most beautiful in the king's sight, and he gave her the crown and she became queen instead of Vashti.

Then — surprise, surprise! — the king gave a great feast to celebrate.

Meanwhile, Mordecai, who was sitting at the king's gate waiting to hear what happened to Esther, overheard two of the king's servants plotting to assassinate the king. Quickly Mordecai told Esther, and quickly Esther warned the king.

"Look out, O King," she said. "Two of your servants are plotting to kill you."

"Oh they are?" said the king. "How ghastly. They must be hanged at once. Thank you very much for the warning."

So they were hanged. And the king was grateful to his new queen.

After picking his new queen, Ahasuerus picked an adviser. He chose a man called Haman.

"You shall be my top adviser, Haman," said the king. "You shall be more important than everyone else except me, and everyone must bow down extremely low whenever they see you."

"Oh, thank you, how marvelous," said Haman. "I love being bowed to."

The king was better at picking queens than advisers, as we shall see.

So everyone bowed whenever Haman passed by. Everyone, that is, except Mordecai. Mordecai didn't because being a Jew, he would bow down only to God. This made Haman absolutely furious, and he determined to get rid not only of Mordecai but of all the Jews in the country, because he hated them.

With this in mind, Haman went to the king and said, "Good morning, O King. Here is my morning's advice. There are some people scattered about in your kingdom who have their own God and their own rules and don't obey your laws properly, which is all rather tiresome. My advice is to get rid of the whole lot of them; they're a nuisance."

The king trusted Haman so much that he never even asked whom he was talking about or what he meant to do to get rid of them!

"Right you are," he said. "Give any instructions you want. Here's my ring to seal them with."

"Thank you, O King," said Haman gleefully, and off he went thinking, "Now I've fixed that wretched Jew Mordecai and the whole lot of them, too."

He spent a happy morning writing letters to all the rulers and governors of all the provinces, telling them on a certain day to slay every single Jew in their province, every man, every woman and every child. Then he sent off the letters and waited happily for the day.

Esther knew nothing at all about all of this because business and politics were seldom discussed with women. But Mordecai knew, and he ripped his clothes and put on sackcloth and ashes. So people came to Esther and said, "Did you know that your uncle is at the gate ripping his clothes?"

"Oh no, how awful. Why?" asked Esther. "Go and find out."

So they went and asked Mordecai why he was ripping his clothes, and they came back with a message.

"Mordecai says that Haman's going to destroy all the Jews in the country, so you must go to the king and get it stopped."

"Oh, my heavens, how appalling," said Esther. "Tell him I can't go to the king unless he sends for me. There's a law that says that anyone who goes to see the king without an invitation will be killed."

Back came Mordecai's message: "Don't be so feeble, girl. After all, you're a Jew yourself, so you'll be killed anyway. So just go to the king."

"All right," said Esther. "Get all the Jews in the city to pray for me for three days, then I'll go to the king."

You would think she would have gone to see her uncle instead of sending messages back and forth, but she wasn't allowed to. Queens were only supposed to talk to the people in their households.

After praying for three days, Esther put on all her best clothes and nervously went and stood by the king's house, hoping the king would be happy to see her and would not angrily have her killed. She stood among all the people who had come to ask a favor of the king.

"Oh, hello, Queen Esther," said the king in surprise. "What on earth are you doing here? Do you want a favor? You can have whatever you want, even half my kingdom if you feel like doing some ruling."

What a relief! Esther breathed freely for the first time in three days.

"Thank you *so* much, O King," she said. "No, I don't actually want to rule. But I'd love it if you and Haman would come to dinner with me tonight."

"That would be delightful," said the king. "Someone send an order to Haman to come to dinner with the queen."

So the king and Haman went to dinner with Esther. And the king said, "That was delicious, my dear. Now is there anything else you'd like?"

"Well," said Esther, "if you wouldn't be bored, I'd love you both to come to dinner tomorrow evening, too."

"Certainly we'll come," said the king. And Haman was very proud because he was the only person invited with the king. But as he left the king's palace, his joy turned to rage because there was Mordecai, who wouldn't stand up or bow or get out of his way.

Haman controlled his temper until he got home. Then he said to his wife, "That arrogant wretch Mordecai. He refuses to bow to me. He's ruined all my pleasure. I was so happy to go to dinner with the queen, then I saw him and felt furious."

"Oh, how annoying for you," said his wife. "Why don't you build a fearfully high gallows outside and ask the king tomorrow if you can hang Mordecai before you go out to dinner?"

"What a good idea," said Haman, and he immediately had a very high gallows built.

Now it so happened that the king couldn't sleep that night, so he decided to pass the time reading the records of all that had happened during his reign. And there he found it written that Mordecai had heard of the plot to assassinate him and had saved his life.

"Oh, by the way," said Ahasuerus to his servants. "What sort of reward did Mordecai get for saving my life? What's been done for him?"

"Oh," they told him, "nothing was done."

"But good gracious, that's terrible," said the king. "Something must be done at once. Which of my advisers is at hand?"

At that very moment Haman came along. He had just finished building the gallows and had come to ask the king about hanging Mordecai.

So Haman came in, and the king said, "Ah, just the man I want, Haman. Now, tell me, what do you think I should do for someone I want to reward? Someone who has done a lot for me."

Haman jumped to the wrong conclusion altogether.

"The king is going to honor and reward me," he thought. "What a marvelous opportunity."

"Let me see," he said to the king. "If you want to reward someone, I think you should give him some of your best clothes to wear and one of your best horses to ride on and one of your spare crowns for his head. And let him ride through the city for everyone to see."

"Splendid," said the king. "See that everything you mentioned is done for Mordecai the Jew."

And of course Haman had to do it, but how he must have hated every minute of it! He went home and told his wife what a miserable day he'd had.

"You'd better look out," said his wife. "Mordecai's clever."

Then messengers came to take Haman to Queen Esther's banquet. And when the feast was over, Ahasuerus said again, "Now, Queen Esther, what would you like me to do for you? Whatever you want you shall have."

"Thank you, O King," said Esther. "You are more than kind. If you really want to please me, I would like you to save my life and the lives of all my people. I am a Jew, and there's an order out throughout your empire to kill us all."

"What?" said the king. "Who has done this thing? How dare anyone send out this order without telling me?"

"That wicked Haman did it," said Esther.

The king was so angry and disappointed in Haman that he went into the garden to calm down. When he came back in, one of his servants said, "There's a huge gallows out there, O King. Why not hang Haman on it? Haman built it to hang Mordecai on, although Mordecai saved your life."

"Hang Haman thereon," said Ahasuerus.

So Haman was hanged on his own gallows.

Then Esther said to the king, "Mordecai is my uncle, you know."

"Oh, is he?" said the king. "Well, let's send for him."

When Mordecai came, the king gave him his ring, which Haman had used.

"Now, Mordecai," said Ahasuerus. "You can be my chief adviser, and you'd better write to all my governors to cancel those wicked orders at once."

So Esther saved the Jews, and they have remembered it every year since then in a feast called Purim.

The Story of Tobit

Among the Israelites taken captive by the Assyrians were a man called Tobit, his wife, Anna, and their son, Tobias. Tobit and Anna continued to remember God and obey the laws, although many of the other captured Jews did not. Tobit always looked after other Jews who were not as well off as he was, and Tobias was strictly brought up to do the same.

One day during the feast of Pentecost, which comes fifty days after Passover, Anna had made an extra good dinner. But before they started it, Tobit said to Tobias, "Go out and see if you can find any poor hungry Jew to come in and share our feast today."

"Yes, all right," said Tobias, and he went out. But he came back in and said, "I can't find any poor, hungry Jews, but I did see a dead Jew in the marketplace whom no one has buried."

"Thank you, Tobias," said Tobit, "that's very sad. But the rules say not to bury anyone until sunset, so I'll do it after dinner."

Dinner was not the jolly meal it was supposed to be, and after dark Tobit went out to bury the dead Jew. Because it was too late to have a bath after he'd finished, and because burying the Jew had made him rather grubby, Tobit thoughtfully slept out of doors. Unfortunately, he didn't realize the garden was full of sparrows, who dropped dirt in his eyes that made him blind. It all seems rather unfair. The doctors couldn't cure him or help at all; so Tobit's family grew very poor, and Anna had to take in washing to make ends meet.

Then one day Tobit remembered that he had left ten talents of silver with a friend of his before the Assyrians came. (A talent is an ancient weight used for money.) So he said to Tobias, "Now that we're rather poor, the ten talents would be most useful. I left them with Gabael in Rages of Media. Would you like to go and get them from him for me?"

"Yes, of course," said the obedient lad. "I'll do anything you want. But how will I get there, and how will I know who Gabael is?"

"Well, why don't you find some sensible, responsible man to go with you," said Tobit, "and I'll pay him some wages."

So out went Tobias, where he at once saw a strange man and said to him, "Could you come with me to find Gabael in Rages?"

"Oh, by all means," said the strange man. "As it happens, I know the way very well and have often stayed with Gabael."

"Oh, what tremendous luck," said Tobias. "Wait a minute while I tell my father."

"Well, hurry up," said the man.

So Tobias told Tobit, but Tobit said, "Good heavens, boy. Bring the man here. You can't go gallivanting off with any old stranger. I must find out who he is and what tribe he belongs to and so on."

So the man came in, and Tobit asked him who he was.

"I'm Azarias, the son of Ananias of your tribe," said the man.

"Oh goodness gracious me, are you really?" said Tobit in amazement. "I knew Ananias well. We used to go to Jerusalem together in the old days. That's splendid. Now what wages would you like? Would a drachma a day do?"

"Yes, that will be fine," said the man. (A drachma is an ancient Greek coin.)

So off they set together. But Anna cried and said to her husband, "Why have you sent off our only son like that? I bet he will never come back again."

"Oh yes he will, my dear," said Tobit. "Don't fret. That good man will take care of him."

So Anna obediently stopped crying.

But as the whole thing seems a lot more unlikely to us than it obviously did to Tobit, we may as well admit that the man was not called Azarias at all. He was really the angel Raphael, but he never told them until the end.

In the evening Tobias and the angel came to a river, and Tobias caught a fish.

"Keep the heart and liver and gall," said Raphael, "and we'll roast the rest."

So they ate roast fish for dinner.

"What good are these little bits we're keeping?" asked Tobias.

"Well," said Raphael, "the heart and liver are very good for smoking out devils, and the gall is useful sometimes for curing blindness."

"Oh," said Tobias.

When they came to Rages, the angel said, "We'll stay with your cousin Raguel. He's got a beautiful daughter called Sara. You ought to marry her, according to the laws."

"Oh dear," said Tobias. "I've heard of Sara. She's been married seven times, but each time her husband died on the wedding night. I don't know that I fancy marrying her all that much. After all, I am my father's only son, and he'd be quite upset if I died."

"Don't worry," said Raphael. "She's meant to be your wife, so all you have to do is burn the fish heart and liver in your bedroom when you marry her, and the smoke will scare the devil away."

So they went in to Raguel's house, and when he opened the door the first thing Raguel said to his wife Edna was, "Here are guests, and one of them is a lad who looks remarkably like Tobit, don't you think? I wonder if he knows Tobit."

"Oh, yes, rather," said Tobias. "Tobit is my father, as a matter of fact."

Then Raguel kissed him and inquired about Tobit and Anna. When they heard that Tobit was blind, they were very sad.

Then Edna made a feast, and Tobias saw that Sara was fearfully pretty and he longed to marry her.

"Oh, but of course," said Raguel. "You can certainly marry her. But I really must warn you that she's been married seven times already, and all her husbands died on the wedding night."

"Oh, never mind," said Tobias. "I'll risk it."

So he risked it and married her, and on the wedding night he burnt the fish heart and liver in their bedroom. This made such a repulsive smell that the devil couldn't stand it, and he fled to the farthest part of Egypt, where an angel tied him up. So that was the end of that little problem, and Tobias didn't die.

But Raguel was so sure that Tobias would die that he got up early the next morning and dug a grave, ready to bury him in, and then went sadly indoors to have breakfast. When Sara and Tobias came to join him, he could scarcely believe his eyes.

"Oh, thank God for that," he said, and sent a servant to fill up the grave because they wouldn't need it after all.

Instead they had the wedding feast for fourteen days, and Raguel said that Tobias could have all his possessions when he died — and half of them then and there. He must have been extremely thankful that his daughter had finally got a live husband.

Raphael didn't stay for all the feasting because Tobias asked him to go to Gabael for the silver so that they could hurry home right after the feast.

"My father will be counting the days until we come home again," said Tobias, "and this feasting takes such an age. My parents will start to worry long before we can get back, I'm afraid."

So Raphael went and got the bags of silver from Gabael and brought them to Tobias.

Tobias was quite right. Tobit was counting the days, and when Tobias should have arrived home and hadn't, Tobit was very worried.

"What's keeping him?" he asked. "Is Gabael dead perhaps, so there's no one to hand over the money? Or what?" And he was very sorry he had sent Tobias.

Then Anna said, "See? What did I tell you? I said this would happen. I bet Tobias is dead and I'll never be happy ever again." And she began to weep and wail. So Tobit quickly backtracked.

"Oh, hold your peace, woman," he said. "Of course Tobias is all right. He'll come."

"Hold your peace, yourself," said Anna. "Tobias is dead, I'm sure he is." So she cried all night and gave up eating meat.

Meanwhile, in Rages, the wedding feast had ended, and Tobias said to his father-in-law, "Look, I really must go home or my parents will think I am dead."

Raguel didn't want him to go, but in the end he agreed and gave him Sara and half his goods, servants, cattle and money, and said, "Well, all right. Have a jolly journey."

And to Sara he said, "Mind you are polite to your father-in-law and mother-in-law so that I hear nice things about you."

Edna said to Tobias, "Be nice to Sara and bring the grandchildren to see us some time."

And at last they set off accompanied by Raphael, of course.

When they were quite close to home, Raphael said to Tobias, "I think we'd better hurry on ahead of Sara and the servants to warn your father that you're married. Otherwise it might be a bit of a shock. And bring that fish gall with you."

So they hurried ahead and the dog went with them. And Anna saw them in the distance and ran as fast as she could to meet them, only pausing to shout to Tobit, "He's coming! Tobias and the man are coming!"

Then she ran and hugged Tobias and wept with pleasure. And Tobias shed a few manly tears as well. But when

Tobit went toward the door to greet them, he almost fell from stumbling into things because of his blindness. So Tobias caught hold of him and at the same time rubbed the fish gall on his eyes.

"Here, what are you doing?" said Tobit. "That hurts." And he rubbed his eyes because they smarted. But when he stopped rubbing, he found that he could see again, and then he wept, too.

Then Tobias told his father about Sara, so when she eventually arrived they had another wedding feast. But this one only lasted for seven days.

After a while Tobit said to Tobias, "What about that man who went with you? What shall we give him?"

"Well, Father," said Tobias, "I should like to give him half of everything I brought back with me, because after all I owe it all to him. Look what he did! He introduced me to my wife, he got the silver from Gabael and he cured you of your blindness."

So they sent for Raphael and Tobit said, "Take half the things Tobias brought with him and have a good journey. I can't thank you enough for what you've done for my son and for me."

"Oh, that's all right," said the angel. "I'm not really Azarias at all. I'm Raphael, one of the seven angels who keep God informed about things. God sent me to bring you a good daughter-in-law and to restore your sight because you have kept all His commandments. I told Him how you buried the dead and how you'd gone blind, and He said I was to cure you. So now I'm going back to God, and you should give thanks to Him, not me, and write the whole story down in a book."

So Tobit said quite a long prayer and wrote the story down in a book.

Tobias and Sara had six sons. When Tobit and Anna were dead, Tobias and Sara took the boys to Media, and they all lived with Raguel and Edna.